The Erotic Cookbook

Cristina Moles Kaupp

f

FUSION PRESS

Publisher's Note

All ingredient quantities for recipes have been provided in metric and US measures. Oven temperatures have been provided in centigrade and Fahrenheit.

First published in Great Britain in 1999 by Vision Paperbacks, a division of Satin Publications Ltd.

Revised edition published 2002 by Fusion Press, a division of Satin Publications Ltd.

© 1998 Deutscher Taschenbuch Verlag, Munich, Germany
© Cover art 1998 Thilo Härdtlein
© English edition 1999 Vision Paperbacks, London
© English edition 2002 Fusion Press, London

Fusion Press
101 Southwark Street
London SE1 0JF
UK
e-mail: info@visionpaperbacks.co.uk
website: www.visionpaperbacks.co.uk

Originally published in Germany in 1998 by Deutscher Taschenbuch Verlag, Munich.

Publisher and translator: Sheena Dewan
Typeset by FiSH Books, London WC1
Printed and bound in the UK by Biddles Ltd
ISBN: 1-901250-27-X

Contents

THE WAY TO A MAN'S HEART IS THROUGH HIS STOMACH

He loves white: his shirt, vest, trousers, even his hat are snow white. He is almost like an old-fashioned dandy out of a book because he has taste as well as a love of life. His wife suits him – she's pure luxury; young, graceful, playful and always smiling. She is lying naked in the hotel bed, half covered by a light sheet. As he stands in the middle of the room he watches her, while pouring champagne into a tall fluted glass.

There is a knock. The hotel boy brings in their food. He stares, embarrassed by the woman's bare breast. Even more champagne, crustaceans and other delicacies... The husband lifts his glass and she winks at him, and gives him that 'come hither' look. A kiss... tender nibble of her earlobe... his tongue licks her smooth armpit and he reaches for the salt cellar. Slowly, he trickles salt over her nipple, and stretches for half the lemon, which smiles at him from the fruit bowl. He squeezes it over her breast. He sucks greedily – salt, lemon, pips, everything. She moans and turns to crawl over him and to the pot of cream. She dips her breast into it and moves back to him, stuffs his mouth full of warm flesh and soft white, which he loves so much. She lies next to him, her fingers in front of his mouth. Is that honey that slowly drips down? It is licked up. Now some red wine. He pours it into a glass bowl, and grabs a small shrimp, still alive, throwing it into the wine. He pours it quickly over his beauty's stomach. A panicking animal tickles her beautiful abdomen in the throes of drunken death.

He stands at the sea and observes a young oyster farmer emerging from the waves. Her pale dress clings to her slight figure. Dripping, she stands before him.

'What did you get out of the sea?' he asks.

She shows him her basket of oysters.

'May I have one?'

She nods, opens one up and offers him the shimmering shell. He takes it and presses it passionately against his mouth. He pulls back, his lip bleeding. Regretfully, he lowers the shell and stares at the girl.

'Can I help you?' She takes the shell and cuts out the flesh – it slips into her wet hand. Searching glances, a drop of blood falls onto the shining oyster flesh. Hastily he gulps it down. He stays, anticipating the aftertaste. So beautifully white, wild black hair, the fresh red on his lips. She can't resist. She reaches up to him and licks his blood in lust.

Scenes from the Japanese film *Tampopo, or the Secret of Noodle Soup* by Juzo Itami.

Many believe that the search for food is more important than the search for a mate and the desire to reproduce – quite logically perhaps, nature places hunger before sexuality.

For some animals, there is an inextricable link between nourishment and reproduction – some spiders, insects and microscopic organisms eat their partner once the sexual deed is done. It may be hard, not to mention desperately immoral, to imagine eating our loved one, but there is no denying the emotional link between love, sex and food. After all, how many lovers say 'I love you so much I could eat you up'?

While not sexual in nature, Catholicism teaches the

doctrine of transubstantiation, the mystical process of the communion bread and wine becoming Christ's body and blood when it is taken at the altar. Christ said 'Take this bread and eat it, for it is my body. Take this wine and drink it, for it is my blood.' And Christ, for Christians, is the highest love of all.

This rite of communion goes back to both the ancient custom of human sacrifice and the belief that the essence of the devoured is somehow absorbed by the eater, who gets as close as possible to them. Such a celebration has inevitable erotic association through the ecstatic desire for unity.

In Greek myth, Artemis ground up the bones of her husband when he died and drank the powder in perfumed water, as she felt there was no better place to keep her loved one than within her body. Many other myths, fairy tales and significant works of literature show a close connection between cannibalism and eroticism, such as *Penthesilea* by Heinrich von Kleist, *Ulysses* by James Joyce and *120 Days of Sodom* by the Marquis de Sade.

Adam and Eve encountered eroticism for the first time when they stole the forbidden apple and exposed their inner selves – their curiosity and readiness to break the rules. They provoked the separation of the table and the bed, and so instilled in our hearts the longing for the unity of one with the other. That eroticism and food are linked and that hunger not only means a longing for food but also sex, has since become universally understood.

Treating A 'Crazy' Condition

The desire to be aroused is in many ways 'irrational', in that it has no bearing on the survival of the individual or the perpetuation of the species in a direct way. And yet, we are obsessed by the pursuit of the fulfilment of our erotic desires. Through the ages, there is barely an animal or plant that has not been used in an elixir or potion in the attempt to increase sexual appetite – in creams, amulets and magic spells.

Animal survival instincts seem to be far more honed than that of humans; for the most part, they are stronger, braver, faster and more fertile. And, they are not distracted by the paradoxes and complexities of sexual gratification. Animals often have sharper senses and frightening weapons at their disposal – horns, claws, poisons, teeth, electric shocks and offensive odours – without having to resort to tools.

Many animals reproduce more frequently than humans, and in many cases, the relative size of animals' sexual organs are more impressive than those of men. Humans have been long impressed by this and as a result have ascribed unique powers of potency and virility to animals. In many myths, the gods disguised themselves as animals: Zeus came to earth as a bull on one occasion, and on another he transformed himself into a horse in order to mate with a nymph who had changed herself into a mare to escape his advances. In other cultures, there is an enduring fear of the power of animals, both real and mythical.

But there is no pharmacological evidence to suggest that animal-based aphrodisiacs increase sexual desire, yet to this day animal horns, testicles and bones are held in high esteem, sometimes causing species to become endangered, or even extinct. There are unfortunately still those who believe that wearing amulets or eating antlers, bull or rhinoceros horn, dried testicles and penises, will pass the sexual desire and strength of the creature on to them.

Sometimes this belief can be deadly – an oil beetle, known in ancient times as cantharis (now confusingly known as 'Spanish fly'), was one of the most popular aphrodisiacs. It contains the poisonous substance cantharidin, and is said to guarantee, when powdered and used in small doses, a huge increase in sex drive. Despite its dangerous side effects – as little as 30mg can be fatal – this green beetle ends up in numerous love potions and creams.

Many believe that certain plants hold aphrodisiacal powers because of their colour, shape or perfume, and in some cases, their poisons. In Greek myth, plants were also imbued with the qualities and personalities of the gods. Zeus lived in the oak tree, and Athena in the olive tree. Pan was embodied in ivy, Wotan in the ash and Hathor, the Egyptian mother of all gods, in the fig tree. The trunk, bark, leaves and fruit of these and other plants were therefore imbued with godly strength and qualities. The roots of these holy plants, bearing deep into the earth, were considered to be conduits for vital earth energy. This energy is expressed through the perfume of the plant. Burning the leaves, stems, flowers and resins of plants is, in many cultures, believed to help free the soul from the body and bring the individual nearer to the realm of the gods. Special secret scents have been passed down since the times of Ancient Egypt. In India, bewitching smoke and aphrodisiac essences such as sandalwood, cinnamon oil or musk are still part of Tantric sexual rituals.

Today, manufactured perfumes are more widely used than natural scents, although their ingredients are derived from plants and animals. When natural animal ingredients are used, some of the most popular aphrodisiac ingredients are glandular sex secretions, produced while the animal is in heat during the breeding season. Castoreum, musk and zibet are all harvested from animals, sometimes with considerable cruelty involved. Nevertheless, most humans find these aromas breathtaking, even though they are illegal in many countries.

In the 1960s and 70s, incense was a common accompaniment to sexual discovery and experimentation in many a teenage bedroom, and nowadays there is renewed interest in natural scents, with the increasing popularity of aromatherapy oils.

Aphrodisiacs in History

According to the Bible, when Adam and Eve gained the knowledge of lust, they were driven from paradise. As humans developed, the centre of awareness shifted from the loins to the brain. We forgot our sense of intuition, and dealt with questions of morality with rationality rather than emotions, intuitions or the unconscious, and it seemed that there was no going back to Eden.

Nevertheless, nature continued to provide helpful hints and signs that man had to both learn and respect; behind the wealth of substances, colours, forms and smells, humans would always suspect that there were hidden codes shrouded in the natural world. If they could be deciphered, perhaps the mysterious relationship between minerals, plants, animals and humans could be revealed. At least, this was the view of the doctor, Paracelsus. He pioneered a new form of medicine in the 16th century, through which medical knowledge was gleaned empirically, purely from observation of nature – 'the body and its purpose is one thing'. He believed every star, every body, every material, element and organ possessed specific qualities, which either attracted or repelled. Sympathy or antipathy, relationship or enmity, positive or negative, these polarities and signs of nature and the stars needed to be explained. This view played an important role in the Middle Ages in explaining the nature of the world, but also in the preparation of medicines and aphrodisiacs.

In those days Europe was relatively sexually liberal, and the Church was for the time being fighting a losing battle against this. In fact the Church unintentionally encouraged free sexuality – the Crusades brought public bathing to Europe, and it was from these baths that brothels emerged. In these public baths everything possible was done to create an erotic atmosphere; they burnt the seeds and leaves of the henbane plant and many stimulating foods and drinks were on the menu.

Ultimately, as a result of increasing political pressure, the Church gained ground in its fight to end such liberties. Everything deemed immodest was prohibited; anything sexual that was not directly concerned with procreation was unacceptable. Highly spiced food and roasted meat were on the index of forbidden foods, as they were believed to incite lust. To guard against wantonness, foods that kept 'the body damp and cold, for instance pumpkins, melons, acetic acid and bitter food, boiled lentils seasoned with vinegar' were favoured (Francesco Rappi, 'New Little Treasure Trove: The Three Chastities', in Piero Campresi's *The Secrets of Venus*).

The most 'passionate' permitted food was a milky vegetable soup with fresh bread and soft egg white, but only for married couples. The egg white was supposed to encourage the man's potency to ensure a happy marriage. But even within marriage, there were many rules: intercourse was only allowed in one position – the missionary position. Other 'indecent' variations could be punished with seven years in jail. Sex was forbidden altogether on certain days: Sundays, Wednesdays and Fridays; 40 days before Easter and Christmas; 40 days after childbirth and three days before communion – at which regular attendance was required, and the confession beforehand acted as a perfect instrument to monitor a couple's observance of the rules.

But the connection between food and sex continued. In the Middle Ages, lovers would have erotic dinners in the bathroom next to the bedroom. Giacomo Casanova regarded it as his right, after a meal, to sleep with his dining companion, which is described in his autobiography *History of My Life*.

In order to survive the Church's 'war on sex', many who felt that their love life needed a boost would seek advice and support from wise women, witches, alchemists and doctors. Ironically, many of the recipes they recommended came from old Church texts. Plants that resembled the human sex organs or whose juice smelt like sperm or vaginal secretions were thought to stimulate sexual appetite. Asparagus, root vegetables, cucumber, morel and carrots simply had to be good for the man's penis; fruits that resembled the vagina, such as apricots, plums and peaches could only kindle the flame of a woman.

The search for effective herbs for love potions continued – it was the devil's and witches' work in some people's view and a gift from heaven for others. The Church responded with monks' research into herbs that would dampen or remove sexual desire altogether. The monk's tree, water lily and the so-called monks' pepper had the reputation of dampening longing, but these plants did not have the desired effect on society.

But the wise women were always one step ahead. They had tinctures that ostensibly reduced the size of breasts and made them firm, methods that made 'worn-out' women younger or that made those who had lost their virginity virgins once more. They knew of magic that could guarantee the love of a particular person or that could tame obstinate people.

It is said that their most famous potion was an 'enticing cream' that when worn would entice the object of one's desire. The exact recipe of this narcotic and psychedelic mixture was not passed down, but it probably contained fats, incense, seasoning, poisons and aphrodisiacs. However, the Church's witch-hunters suspected it contained human fat and boiled babies, dragon's blood and devil's dirt.

In the Middle Ages and the Renaissance, alchemists and the Sympathy school revived herbalism, but they were also interested in human organs, using Paracelsus' theory: 'The most effective medicine for humans is man.' Italian astrologer Girolamo Manfredi agreed: 'There is no food that would be more acceptable as nourishment for humans than human flesh, if nature hadn't made it so repulsive.'

It is said that some witches used parts of the human body in some of their medicines: the heart, eyes, sexual organs, liver and kidneys. As recently as the 19th century, the body parts of executed people were considered to contain magical powers. In ancient times the liver was thought to be the seat of the soul and was supposed to be the repository of wisdom and sexual energy. Penises and fingers sold very well as 'thieves' candles'. The fat from poor sinners and babies' blood was added to an assortment of creams designed to guard against impotence.

In the 18th and 19th centuries, Egyptian mummies were brought to Europe, and some were used in apothecaries' tinctures – they were believed to have aphrodisiac qualities. A pharmacist from Dresden in Germany, E. Merk, offered 'Mumia vera aegyptica' in his catalogue for 17.50 marks per kilo – a fortune in those days. Other aphrodisiacs of the time included unlikely ingredients such as mother's milk, ear wax, urine, excrement, secretions from the foreskin glands or sperm itself. Those who find this revolting and are glad not to have lived in those times should remember that some beauty creams, even today, contain human placenta. It is uncertain whether some of these controversial methods had any therapeutic value, but certain ancient healing modalities, such as urine therapy, are making a comeback.

The Kama Sutra

Tantra shows that one doesn't need to go to such extreme lengths to secure a satisfactory love life. *The Kama Sutra* teaches that sexual satisfaction is of particular importance for both men and women, which runs contrary to the teachings of most Churches in the West – even today. According to the Christian Church, women had no right to their own sexuality, let alone a satisfying one. This view is, however, changing. In *The Kama Sutra*, sexual partners were sorted into special categories according to the size of their sexual organs: men in buck, bull and stallion, the women in gazelle, mare and elephant-cow. For sexual intercourse, the love-book has 64 positions, which are poetically described in detail. Sado-masochistic practices, the use of dildos, and male homosexual practices were all integrated in the sex games, although interestingly lesbianism was not permitted. *The Kama Sutra* also recommended recipes for love potions, a mixture of cosmetics, medicine and magic.

The Tantrists passed on many rituals and recipes for increasing sexual pleasure and psychic powers. Students of Tantra learn details about sexual behaviour that are often not understood in the Western culture and are even considered pornographic. Yet their rituals serve to blend the masculine and feminine principles to restore their original unity. This bodily, spiritual and mental unification is supposed to reveal to the human his or her origins, so that one can be enlightened and rediscover Godliness.

From Longing To Enjoyment

How simple it would all be if there were a perfect aphrodisiac. It could be a little magic pill that makes one irresistible, or a drop of a bewitching scent that confuses our senses. How alluring it would be to sprinkle a pinch of some powder into our partner's food – perhaps after years of being together – and after a few mouthfuls they suddenly become expert in a variety of new erotic delights; shivers of lust through the whole body; orgasms that last much longer – it would be Utopia. We've been trying to find this place for centuries.

Modern love is dictated by speed. Few who are plagued by stress have time for prolonged sex. The pressure of modern life leads to 'quickies' and one-night-stands that lack fantasy. We expect aphrodisiacs to work with a correspondingly quick kick and visible success, and we therefore often turn to drugs, such as alcohol and Viagra. Those who don't mind taking illegal drugs may try cannabis, LSD and cocaine.

Despite many impotence preparations, supplements and Spanish fly, there is no such thing as the perfect aphrodisiac. But there are a number of plants that have narcotic effects, seasonings that stimulate, smoking herbs that excite and many other ingredients. Perhaps one should view aphrodisiacs with the attitude 'the journey is the destination'. It could be argued that the simple belief in an aphrodisiac can go a long way to making it effective – a case of 'mind over matter'. This book is designed to highlight the sensual connection between food and eroticism, the longing for it and the yearning for even more.

The aphrodisiac market is mostly aimed at men, because when passion fails, the signs are more noticeable. Moreover, it has only become acceptable in recent years for women to demand more from their sex lives. 'Hence I stumble from longing to enjoyment, and in the enjoyment I pine for longing', commented Johann Wolfgang von Goethe. He was not the first to write about the paradox of desire; whether nibbling or feasting, whether secretly or openly, trying strange or forbidden things promises titillation. Lust, at least in our fantasies, is the realm of the wildest dreams and the most insatiable longings.

When it comes to lust-filled foods, they never seem to be homemade – temptation always seems to come from outside. The surprise meal out, the exotic and enticing delicacies and tempting little dishes...clever or simple, piquant or classical...there are so many cuisines to entice your lover. Italian, French, Japanese...whatever it is, timing and presentation are paramount.

A small, carefully composed three-course gourmet menu that is high in vitamins and minerals, seasoned fresh herbs and light sauces, a *diner à deux*, can be a temptation par excellence, and a large banquet can work wonders.

Love, whether physical or emotional, is not, never was and never will be simple. The door to the Garden of Eden remains closed. But through the romantic dinner, perhaps we can peek through the crack in the door of Paradise.

Aphrodisiacs

Aphrodite – Goddess of Love

It was no ordinary sea-foam that gave birth to Aphrodite, the Greek Goddess of love and temptation. She was born out of the foam that was created when Uranus' castrated penis was thrown into the sea. Uranus was the god of the sky, and Gaia was the goddess of the Earth. Theirs was a difficult union, but they had 12 children – six male and six female Titans. But all their offspring were so deformed that Uranus stamped 11 of them into the earth. When their last son, Kronos, was born, Gaia swore to get revenge for Uranus' rejection of her children. She sent Kronos away to be given a safe upbringing, and when he became an adult, he returned. She gave him a sickle so that he could remove Uranus' manhood, to prevent him from approaching her sexually ever again. The time came, and Kronos castrated his father. The god's mighty penis was thrown into the sea, and from the spot it landed, the Goddess of Love was born.

'Aphro' means foam. The waves played over the severed phallus and, out of the foaming 'sperm', Aphrodite appeared – beautiful, perfect in stature and movement, and sensuous down to her last detail. A clam shell carried the naked beauty to the shores of Cyprus in a floating procession accompanied by sparrows and doves. Roses blossomed on her arrival; wherever she trod, flowers and scented herbs sprouted. The island turned into a sea of flowers and even wild animals became gentle when they saw her.

Hesiod described Aphrodite as 'one who was the laugh of lovers [actually: the genitals of those who would like to love], because she was created from the genital parts'. The goddess 'bore a longing for love in her breast and she went straight away to the shade of the valley to mate', Homer sang. She even caused Zeus to lose his mind and managed to get him to 'willingly couple with mortal women'. Sexual excess, misunderstanding, confusion, erotic aberrations between animals, humans and gods – Aphrodite managed it all.

She owned a magic belt that was filled with every ingredient possible for the kindling of love and raising of sexual desire, as well as the art of temptation and potency. In order to have access to her aphrodisiacs, the Greeks built a temple for Aphrodite and begged for her favour. As offerings, they brought her birds, above all sparrows and pigeons, as well as prolific hares and the randy stag. They smothered her statue with scented flowers and herbs, pomegranates, quinces, roses, mint and myrrh. And they feasted in her name on strong, intoxicating drinks and tasty food.

From Nature's Womb To The Kingdom of The Senses

Angel's trumpet: Angel's trumpet is a plant used by Native Americans in shamanic healing rituals. This plant has hallucinogenic properties caused by the tropane alkaloids found in all parts of the plant.
Where found: South America and Europe.
Available from: The seeds can be bought in specialist herbalists, and the plant is found growing in many European gardens.
How to use: Brew the seeds in water or wheat beer and drink.
Effect: Strong narcotic, hallucinations – use with care.

Aniseed: This healing plant is a popular aphrodisiac and has many culinary uses. It has been used since Greek and Roman times. Aniseed contains pleasant aromatic oils that not only improve food and drink, but also make them healthier. It was believed that men who washed with aniseed retained their youthful appearance.

'Aniseed brings women milk and increases their desire to be immodest' (Leonhard Fuchs, *New Herbal Book*, 1543).
Indigenous to: Europe, especially Eastern Mediterranean.
Where found: Good delicatessens will have fresh aniseed, but it is widely available in dried form.
How to use: Use as a seasoning and healing aid (fresh or dried) in drinks and food.
Effect: Encourages digestion, stimulates the nervous system and alleviates cramps.

Asparagus: Because of its phallus-shaped spears, asparagus is thought to have a stimulating and aphrodisiac effect. The Chinese use asparagus to alleviate coughs; the Egyptians value it as a food and the Greeks as a medicine for the kidneys.
Where found: Worldwide. It is traditionally a seasonal plant, growing in early spring, which is a further reason why it is considered to be an aphrodisiac.
How to use: Asparagus is best steamed, or used in soup.
Effect: Diuretic.

Aubergine (eggplant): Due to its full, round shape, the aubergine, along with other members of the nightshade family, is considered an aphrodisiac. In Italy it is said that the aubergine can rob the eater of his sanity.
Where found: South-east Asia, Mediterranean.

Obtainable from: Widely available in supermarkets throughout the year
How to use: As a vegetable.
Effect: Enlivening and invigorating.

Avocado: Avocados probably originate from the Yucatan Peninsula in Mexico. There is evidence that the ancient Maya people cultivated the trees. Although no aphrodisiac effect has been demonstrated, both the stone (in the form of avocado oil) and the flesh are thought to be sexually stimulating. In addition, the avocado plays an important role in Native American traditional medicine, as a treatment for fevers, herpes and gynaecological problems.
Where found: Central America, tropical and sub-tropical regions, Southern Europe.
Obtainable from: Food shops around the year.
How to use: As a fruit or vegetable, especially in salads and dips.
Effect: Energising and revitalising.

Basil: There are many varieties of basil, and some are better suited to culinary uses, others to medicinal use. *Ocimum sanctum*, a variety found in India, is considered a holy plant for some Hindus, who according to their religion should eat one leaf a day. *Ocimum basilicum* (sweet basil) stimulates the sex drive and boosts fertility, and produces a general sense of well-being through essential oils, tannins and vitamins found in the leaves.
Where found: South Asia and Southern Europe.
Obtainable from: Basil is widely available as a dried herb, although fresh basil is always better. It can be grown in a sunny garden, or bought in most supermarkets.

How to use: As a seasoning, brewed as a tea, smoked (in dried form).
Effect: Stimulating.

Belladonna (poisonous – for reference only): In the past, belladonna was considered to be a very powerful and magical plant. Wiccan witches would prepare highly effective love potions and wines from the belladonna root. Belladonna means 'beautiful woman', and when taken, the atropine in this plant causes the pupils to dilate, which is a sign of arousal.
Where found: Europe, West Asia and North Africa.
Obtainable from: Wild plants grow in woodlands; seeds can be obtained from herbalists or head shops.
How to use: Belladonna can be eaten as a fruit, or the leaves can be smoked. Important note: the entire plant contains alkaloids, including atropine, which in the correct dosage can increase sexual excitement. However, too much can lead to breathing difficulties, and even death. The fatal dose of atropine for humans is 0.1g, and it should be appreciated that it can be difficult to judge the correct number of berries to take, as atropine levels may vary between different berries, so this information is for reference only.
Effect: Strong aphrodisiac and causes hallucinations; death with a high dose.

Betel nut: The seeds of the areca nut palm are widely enjoyed in Asia, both as a food and as a medicine. Betel nuts are most commonly eaten in a *paan* – the nut is grated, and is placed into a fresh betel leaf along with an assortment of other spices such as nutmeg, cloves and pepper with lime. This is then chewed for around 10 minutes, but not normally swallowed.

Where found: South-east Asia and other tropical areas.
Obtainable from: The leaves, nuts and powder can be found in Asian food shops and in head shops.
How to use: Roll the nut up in a *paan*, use as a seasoning, or use the powder in a tea.
Effect: Reduces stress, anti-bacterial, stimulates and enlivens.

Calmus: Since olden times the roots of the calmus plant, which is similar to a reed, have been used in medicinal baths and have been smoked. Traditionally, Native Americans would chew calmus to relieve fatigue, or they would powder it and take it as a snuff. Calmus contains a substance similar to mescaline, called isoasarone. In high doses, calmus is a known aphrodisiac. The roots are collected in spring and late autumn and are then washed and dried. They should be stored in a cool, dry place, and can be used for up to a year after being harvested.
Where found: Originally in Southern Asia, today worldwide.
Obtainable from: Grows wild on the banks of ponds and slow-running rivers; dried roots can be purchased from herbalists (Western or Chinese) or head shops.
How to use: As a snack (roots, doses between 5–25 cm (2–10 in) length of root), or added to tea or alcohol.
Effect: Stimulating, hallucinogenic. A bath with calmus powder added to the water can be an effective aphrodisiac.

Cardamom: Even in ancient times cardamom was used as a herb, healing agent and aphrodisiac. Cardamom is related to the ginger family of plants, and the seeds are used together with the seed pod, which contains the essential oils.
Where found: South-east Asia.

Obtainable from: Most supermarkets in dried form, and fresh in Asian shops.
How to use: As a spice in cooking, or added to coffee.
Effect: Stimulates and enlivens.

Carrot: The carrot has been associated with stimulation since ancient times because of its vitamin content, and of course because of its shape. In Asia carrots are eaten as a substitute for ginseng.
Where found: Worldwide.
Obtainable from: Widely available in food shops, and can be grown in the garden at home.
How to use: As a vegetable (raw or cooked) or as a juice.
Effect: Raises energy levels, encourages sexual intercourse, diuretic.

Celery: Valued as a foodstuff, celery is also known as an aphrodisiac in Europe. Celery roots are said to increase sexual stamina and celery root salad is supposed to work wonders on impotence.
Where found: Worldwide.
Obtainable from: Food shops.
How to use: As a vegetable, seasoning (using celery seeds).
Effect: Stimulant.

Chilli: A variety of paprika that is used as both a vegetable and seasoning, chilli is an integral part of Indian and Asian cuisine. Chilli is considered a 'hot' food, not just because of its taste, but also because it stimulates sexual urges. Capsaicin, the substance that makes chilli hot, irritates and stimulates the mucous membranes, which increases vaginal secretions.

Where found: Central and South America.
Obtainable from: Widely available from supermarkets and delicatessens.
How to use: As a seasoning, but be careful not to use too much!
Effect: Stimulating.

Cinnamon: 2,800 years ago, cinnamon was first mentioned in a Chinese emperor's herbal book. The dried rind of the cinnamon tree is used to season sweet dishes and mulled wine. Thick, spicy-smelling cinnamon oil is distilled from the rind and leaves, and is used to guard against colds. A little cinnamon oil rubbed onto the genitals produces a very strong aphrodisiacal effect.
Where found: South-east Asia.
Obtainable from: Supermarkets.
How to use: As a seasoning in food and drinks. The oil can be added to a hot bath and can also be rubbed into the skin.
Effect: Powerful antibacterial agent, encourages the appetite, regulates the menstrual cycle.

Cloves: The dried green flowers of the clove have been used as an aphrodisiac for well over 5,000 years. The Chinese used to chew cloves before lovemaking, to ensure pleasant breath. Clove oil contains eugenol, which has a mildly psychedelic effect. Cloves also have narcotic and antiseptic qualities; it is still used to protect against mild toothache.
Where found: Cultivated in tropical zones.
Where obtainable: Food shops.
How to use: As a seasoning or oil.
Effect: Stimulating.

Coca: The leaves of the coca bush were widely used in Peru, long before Incan times. Cocaine is derived from the leaves, and is used in the West as a sensory stimulant and euphoric. Used on a localised part of the body, cocaine or coca leaf paste has a numbing effect. Anal intercourse was not considered to be 'unnatural' in Peru, but was practised by both homosexual and heterosexual partners; coca paste was rubbed onto the anus beforehand. Coca was used medicinally as an analgesic, against mountain sickness and as an appetite suppressant. It is still widely used today, and many South Americans prepare the leaves with ash and dissolved lime and chew the leaves.

In 1863, the Corsican chemist, Angelo Mariani, patented a drink made from wine and coca leaves. Twenty-three years later the pharmacist, John S. Pemberton from Georgia, developed a refreshing, stimulating drink, which was to become the symbol of the Western world: Coca-Cola. However, the extract of cola nut and coca leaves have long been removed from the ingredient list and have been replaced by a higher dose of caffeine.

Following Sigmund Freud's publication of his experiments with coca in 1884, snorting cocaine became quite fashionable in European artist circles. However, cocaine is addictive, and not all users would share Gottfried Benn's enthusiasm for how cocaine causes the 'sweet disintegration of the individual'. Many users suffer from depression following the 'come down'. Cocaine no longer enjoys a romantic image, but it is widely used illegally throughout the West.

Where found: South America.

Obtainable from: Cocaine is illegal, and cannot be legally possessed, bought or sold.

How to use: Cocaine powder is snorted, and the coca leaves can be chewed.
Effect: Very strong stimulant and aphrodisiac.

Cocoa: It was the 'nourishment of the Gods' according to the Indians and a much-loved aphrodisiac. The Aztecs grated the roasted beans, mixed the cocoa powder with maize flour, chilli, vanilla, pimento, matico-pepper, rolls of cinnamon bark and pumpkin seeds, and added hot or cold water. Either salted or sweetened with honey, they formed a chocolate. Rococo Europe valued chocolate: 'One obtained strength from chocolate for certain tasks', said a text from the 17th century. Cocoa contains theobromine, which is related to caffeine.
Where found: Central America, Asia, Africa.
Obtainable from: Food shops.
How to use: As a drink (grated beans) and in cooking.
Effect: Slightly stimulating.

Coconut palm: The coconut palm is a very useful plant – not only is the fruit (coconut) edible, but the roots are used for medicinal purposes and palm wine can be tapped from the flower stems. One palm can produce 400 litres of juice in a week, and in many parts of the world this juice is believed to have aphrodisiac qualities. Its effect is enhanced by adding apple seeds and honey. Soft coconut flesh is also supposed to have a stimulating effect.
Where found: Throughout the tropics.
Obtainable from: Food shops (coconuts); Asian shops (milk and palm wine).
How to use: As fruit and as palm wine.
Effect: Strengthens and intoxicates.

Coffee: The brew made from roasted coffee beans was once a holy drink; due to its stimulating effects, it was used by African Sufis during meditation.
Where found: East Africa, Arabia.
Obtainable from: Food shops.
How to use: Brew freshly ground coffee as a drink; do not use instant powder. If being used as an aphrodisiac, coffee can be spiced up with honey and cardamom.
Effect: Powerfully enlivening.

Coriander (cilantro): This herb was well known in olden days in Egypt and Palestine as an effective aphrodisiac. As a seasoning in wine, coriander was thought to increase sperm production.
Where found: Worldwide.
Obtainable from: Most food shops as a powder; seeds and fresh in Asian shops.
How to use: As a seasoning (seeds and leaves).
Effect: Enlivening.

Cress: All edible types of cress – watercress, garden cress and Indian cress – have a high vitamin C content and so help to maintain general well-being. Indian cress' reputation as an aphrodisiac is based purely on the distinct colouring of its leaves.
Where found: Worldwide.
Obtainable from: Food shops.
How to use: As a salad or greens.
Effect: Energy giving.

Date palm: Five thousand years ago, in Mesopotamia, the date palm was cultivated and used as food and as a drug. Juice was

tapped from the stem, which would, after a while, become an intoxicating drink. Probably mixed with other drugs, this drink was served at temple dances and erotic rituals.
Where found: Asia Minor, Arabia, North Africa.
Obtainable from: Food shops as a fruit; as date wine in Asian shops.
How to use: As a fruit, as date wine.
Effect: Energy giving, intoxicating.

Fennel: Fennel originated from the Mediterranean area and was grown by the Romans and Greeks for medicinal and culinary purposes. In the Middle Ages, fennel was said to possess magical aphrodisiac qualities. In medicine it was used for improving eyesight and to guard against indigestion.
Where found: Worldwide.
Obtainable from: Own garden, bulbs in food shops, seeds in specialist herb shops.
How to use: As seasoning (seeds), as greens (leaves), as a vegetable (bulb).
Effect: Refreshing, filling.

Figs: For centuries the fig has been considered a symbol of fertility, due to its form and amount of seeds. It is no coincidence that the fig leaf has been used to cover the genitals of those embarrassed by their nakedness.
Where found: Mediterranean area, sub-tropical and tropical regions.
Obtainable from: Food shops.
How to use: As a fruit (fresh or dried), or as juice.
Effect: Refreshing.

Garlic: Garlic was thought of in ancient Egypt as a healing aid that worked wonders and at the same time acted as a stimulant. The Romans dedicated it to Ceres, the Goddess of Fertility. Mixed with coriander, garlic juice was served as a love potion to cure impotence caused by witchcraft and to encourage illicit liaisons. However, the unpleasant breath that results from eating garlic is enough to make close contact repellent for some people.

'He who during the battle of love cannot prove himself to be a man eats onions and is then really strong. If an elderly woman is tired, then she does not hesitate to eat onions as well, and the gentle Venus will laugh about your battle in a friendly way.' *Roman quotation*
Where found: Worldwide.
Obtainable from: Food shops.
How to use: As a herb (raw, cooked or crushed), tincture or tablet.
Effect: Makes one feel younger, strengthens, antibiotic properties, activates cells.

Ginger: Ginger is a tropical and subtropical cultivated plant, resembling reeds (which are also sold as a healing agent). The roots contain an essential oil, which gives it its characteristic spicy flavour. In Arabian countries, coffee is often spiced up using ginger.
Where found: Southern Asia.
Obtainable from: Food shops.
How to use: As a herb (fresh or dried, as powder, pressed, grated or preserved in syrup), as a refreshing drink (ginger ale), beer or liqueur.
Effect: Enlivens, encourages digestion, stimulates.

Ginseng: The ginseng root (Chinese: human root) is considered the oldest and most sought-after aphrodisiac and healing agent in Asia. As far back as 2500 BC, the doctor Shen-Nung used its enormous powers. In medicine, it has lost none of its value even today. In Chinese healing, harmonising medicines are preferred. Influenced by the Taoist school, it is thought that both of the cosmic powers (Yin (female) and Yang (male)) must become equal, in order to prevent sickness and malfunctioning of the human body. As a general healing aid this 'root of the heavens' is supposed to assist in acquiring eternal life.

However, it is not suitable for the quick kick – the effect of ginseng unfolds only when taken regularly over a long period of time. For spontaneous reactions one has other items ready: ginseng, taken with musk, opium (illegal of course), prawn powder and ginger. He who makes pills from these and chews one half an hour before coitus 'will experience a true wonder'.

Its root form is highly efficacious. It is said that the more it resembles the penis the more explosive the effect, although ginseng is not commonly found in this form. Experienced ginseng hunters also know the rituals and legends connected with this plant: a spirit, in human form, is supposed to live in every root and it unites erotically with the collector. Only the collector knows how he must handle the plant demons, whether to praise them or be cunning, by chanting prayers or magic sayings. Different forms have different effects – check before using.

The Chinese character for ginseng is the same as for potency.
Where found: East Asia.
Obtainable from: Fresh from Asian shops; as tablets, tincture or extract in chemists or drugstores.

How to use: Fresh – either chewed or as tea. Some people place ginseng extract in alcohol for at least three months before using.
Effect: Universal healing agent, strengthens and stimulates if taken regularly.

Guarana: The seeds of this liana vine are also called 'fruits of youth'. It makes a refreshing drink, which is a powerful stimulant. The seeds contain caffeine, resin and an as yet barely researched essential oil.
Where found: The Amazonian basin.
Obtainable from: Health food shops, head shops.
How to use: As a drink (boil the seeds), tincture, chewing gum, chocolate, paste.

Hemp: Hemp is one of the oldest plants known to humanity, and is used as a source of fibre and oil. It is also used to produce hashish and marijuana. The psychoactive effect associated with marijuana is caused by the THC (tetrahydrocannabinol) content of the plant, along with other cannabinoids. Among many users, cannabis has the reputation of being one of the best aphrodisiacs in the world.

The 'grass of ecstasy' is described in Indian religious scripts as a holy plant that not only helps to alleviate physical complaints, but also refreshes the mind and soul. As long ago as 5,000 years, doctors used hemp against various ailments: lack of appetite, headaches, digestion problems and impotence. Its erotic importance is described in the legend about the godly pair, Shiva and Parvati. Shiva, much to the dismay of his wife, played around with other goddesses. During the search for something to bind her husband to her, she discovered the female hemp flower with its resin. She gave it to Shiva to smoke, who was filled with a new lust for his wife. Their heavenly ecstasy was so powerful that from then on Shiva resisted all other temptations.

'The spirit of hemp is the spirit of peace and knowledge. During hemp-induced ecstasy, the lightening of eternity transforms the darkness of martyrdom into pure light.' Hemp is the 'giver of pleasure', 'the seventh heaven', 'heaven's leader', the 'heaven for the poor man', the 'comforter of mourning'. 'No God, no person is as good as the religious hemp drinker', were some of the verdicts of the British Hemp Drug Commission Report, in 1884.

Cannabis is used in drinks for Tantric love rituals. As with opium, the effect varies according to whether one smokes, eats or drinks the plant. For most recipes there are several cannabis drugs at one's disposal: the dried female flower ('marijuana'), the resin from the flowers ('hashish'), fresh or dried leaves ('grass').

Ayurveda (meaning 'knowledge of life') is an ancient Indian school of medicine that recommended blends of hemp buds and other healing ingredients. One such recipe calls for hemp buds and leaves, hashish, opium and thorn apple. This mixture would then be added to various spices including cloves, cardamom, incense, aniseed, caraway seeds, butter fat, flour, milk and sugar.

Where found: Worldwide.

How to use: As an addition to food or as tea (resin), smoked (female flowers).

Note: As a narcotic, hemp is an illegal drug.

Effect: Mildly psychedelic, intensifies awareness, stimulates, increases appetite and sexual desire.

Henbane (poisonous – for reference only): This poisonous nightshade plant has been known since ancient times as a healing plant and was used in magic. Witches brewed amorous love potions from this highly effective plant containing tropane alkaloids. Henbane seeds and leaves would be smoked as an alleged cure for toothache, and in the Middle Ages it was smoked as a stimulant by those visiting 'bathing houses'. Henbane could also be ground up and added to beer.
Where found: Eurasia, North Africa.
Obtainable from: Specialist herb shops and head shops, and can be found growing in the wild.
How to use: Smoke (leaves and seeds).
Note: Eating the seeds is not recommended, as the alkaloids contained in them can be fatal in high doses. Because henbane is a natural substance, the amount of alkaloids found in the seeds can vary from plant to plant.
Effect: Reduces sexual inhibition, hallucinations and vivid dreams.

Honey: Honey is crucial to most aphrodisiac drinks. The Maya Indians would add honey to nightshade, or to various barks, or even to the extracts of toads, which have psychoactive properties. In Mexico, the honey of the stingless bee was a popular aphrodisiac, and in England, mead (honey wine) with extra honey added was regularly taken to increase the libido. Many products are derived from honey, including royal jelly and propolis, which are considered to have many healing properties, including guarding against sterility and impotence.
Where found: Worldwide.
Obtainable from: Food shops.
How to use: On bread, or as mead.

Effect: Stimulates and strengthens.

Horseradish: Horseradish has been grown since the 12th century and is mainly used as a herb. Due to the root's resemblance to a penis, and its use as a spicy seasoning, horseradish was credited with magic powers to prevent sexual exhaustion in men.
Where found: Europe.
Obtainable from: Food shops, and can be grown in one's garden.
How to use: As a seasoning.
Effect: Enlivens and strengthens. Also stimulates digestion.

Liquorice: Liquorice contains, among other things, glycyrrhizin, essential oils and hormones, which are used as an old folk remedy to cure coughs, stomach and bowel problems. It is said to be an aphrodisiac that stimulates women in particular.
Where found: South-east Europe and South-west Asia.
Obtainable from: Asian shops and supermarkets.
How to use: As a powder or tea.
Effect: General tonic.

Lovage: The aphrodisiac effects of the leaves and roots of lovage have been known since ancient times. Love potions can be prepared from lovage roots.
Where found: Eurasia.
Obtainable from: Specialist herbal shops and can be grown in one's garden.
How to use: As seasoning or fresh as salad.
Effect: Enlivening and calming.

Mandrake: The effects of mandrake were discovered by the naturalist Paracelsus. It is a highly sought-after and rare plant.

The roots are supposed to have magic powers; they were often used in magic and heathen rituals. Where the root was found, and what condition it was in, would determine what magic use the root would be put to. In the Middle Ages, it was considered to be dangerous to harvest the roots; it was believed that if a layperson pulled the roots out of the ground, the roots would emit a blood-curdling scream, which would kill the collector on the spot. To counteract this 'danger', a 'black, hungry dog' would be tied to the root with a string. In the dog's attempt to free itself, it would pull the root out, and if there were any danger, the dog would die rather than the harvester.

Whether as a drink, cream or talisman, its narcotic effect made the mandrake very popular. Many legends surround the root, which is also called mandragora (Persian for 'love herb'). 'This magical mandrake/was grown by God and his saviour's forgotten people/under the gallows and strung-up victims/it is said that after death of the hanged/the urine and seeds grew/in the form of a little penis' (Acorn, *The Knowledge of Magic*, 1674).

Mandrake has an anthropomorphic form. With a bit of imagination, one can make out both female and male sex organs. The Church, not surprisingly, viewed the plant as a threat and so damned and banned the plant; they saw potential for a pact with the Devil in the yearning for mandrake and the desire associated with it. In Joan of Arc's trial, reference was made to a talisman made from mandrake, which was worn by the brave Frenchwoman. Superstitions surrounding mandrake demanded scrupulous personal care – in order to keep the volatile spirit of the mandrake in good humour, it was thought that one should change one's clothes regularly and wash the roots in wine.

Originally mandrake grew in the Near East, and the first recipes came from Papyrus. Next to deadly nightshade, henbane and the thorn apple, it was mixed into various love potions, including some enjoyed by Cleopatra. He who could not find the magical plant in Northern Europe, made do with *allemann's* root (Latin: *allumm victorialis*), yellow gentian or Virginia creeper. The roots of all these plants contain highly powerful tropane alkaloids. Possible unpleasant side effects when eating this plant are nausea and a dry mouth.

Where found: Southern Europe, North Africa, Himalayan regions, Asia Minor.

Obtainable from: Specialist herbalists, head shops and occasionally from garden centres.

How to use: As a wine and a tea (a quarter to half a teaspoon of the root is considered to be a safe dose). The leaves can also be smoked.

Caution: In rare cases, overdoses can be fatal as a result of respiratory paralysis.

Effect: Lowers sexual inhibitions, stimulates and is mildly hallucinogenic.

Morels: These mushrooms have been appreciated as aphrodisiacs for centuries in all cultural circles. This could be due to the resemblance they bear to a penis, but is more likely to do with their musky, smoky flavour. One can recognise a morel by its cap, which is full of little holes and resembles a sponge.

Where found: Grows throughout the world during the spring in mountainous regions.

Obtainable from: Food shops and delicatessens, either fresh, dried or preserved.
How to use: As a vegetable.
Effect: Enlivens and sensitises.
Mountain rush: This plant was used in The Netherlands in ancient times as a central part of rituals. In China, the ephedrine plant (Ma-Huang) was an important natural medicine. Nearly every culture is aware of the aphrodisiac effects of tea made from the leaves of the plant.
Where found: Worldwide.
Obtainable from: Chemists, specialist herb shops.
How to use: As greens, tea (15–30g ($^1/_2$–1oz) per litre of water, boil for 10 minutes).
Effect: Enlivens, helps breathing, anti-allergic, stimulates.

Muira puama (Latin – Ptychopetaium olacoides*):* South American Indians have known about this bushy tree for centuries, and it has been used as an aphrodisiac since its discovery. The bark and hard wood are boiled for hours to produce a love potion.
Where found: The Amazon basin.
Obtainable from: Head shops, in the form of an alcohol extract.
How to use: As a drink.
Effect: Extreme excitement, strengthens the nerves, increases potency.

Muscatel sage: This sage has been known since ancient times as a herb and healing aid. Mixed with wine, it increases sexual enjoyment. In aromatherapy, essential oil of sage, whose flavour is similar to amber, acts as an aphrodisiac if inhaled several times a day or if a few drops are taken internally.

Where found: Mediterranean regions.
Obtainable from: Specialist herb shops.
How to use: As a herb or as an essential oil. The dried leaves can be used pure or mixed with henbane, hemp or thorn apple and then smoked.
Effect: Sexually stimulating.

Mustard: Since olden times, mustard has been touted as being able to increase one's potency. The Roman Plinius was convinced that if three leaves of the white mustard were picked with the left hand, then drunk in honey-water, it would increase sexual desire. It was forbidden for monks to eat mustard, as it was feared that the plant would lead them into temptation. There are three types of mustard: black, Indian and white. Black mustard has the most intense aroma.
Where found: Eurasia and North Africa.
Obtainable from: Food shops, and can be grown in one's garden.
How to use: As a seasoning (seeds or paste).
Effect: Stimulating, irritant.

Nettles: For centuries, the nettle was known for its healing and nutritious properties even though the hairs on the leaves contain an irritating poison. In olden days, partners would whip each other with nettle plants to stimulate each other. The Roman poet Petronius maintained that men would retain their masculinity if they rubbed nettles on their navel, loins and buttocks.
Where found: Worldwide.
Obtainable from: One's own garden or growing wild, herbalists and chemists.
How to use: Drink the leaves as a tea or dry them and smoke them

in a rolled cigarette. The fresh leaves can be used as a substitute for spinach in casseroles (young, fresh leaves and stalks).
Effect: Stimulates the circulation, skin irritant (fresh leaves).

Nutmeg: Nutmeg is not really a nut but is actually a seed. Because of the stimulating sensory effects of this spice, it has been considered one of the most popular seasonings since the 16th century. Nutmeg has a psychoactive effect, which lasts up to 12 hours (taking effect between one and five hours after consumption), due to the high level of myristicin in the essential oils found in the seed. A bath with a few drops of nutmeg essential oil has a particularly stimulating effect. Myristicin forms the main basis for the fashionable synthesised drug MDMA (Ecstasy).
Where found: Asia, Africa, cultivated in all tropical zones.
Obtainable from: Food shops as a nut or fresh from Asian shops. The essential oil can be found in health food shops.
How to use: As a spice, or as an essential oil in massage oil or in a bath. Dried, powdered nutmeg can also be smoked in a joint along with hemp.
Effect: Psychoactive, stimulating. Can be dangerous in large quantities.

Onions: The onion is one of the oldest cultivated vegetables and was one of the staple foods of the ancient Egyptians, who treated it as a holy plant. When the Israelis fled from Egypt, they missed onions more than anything else from their diet. For the Greeks and Romans the onion was a medicinal vegetable, a cure for coughs and colds. Onions were as highly esteemed as garlic, as each was believed to be an aphrodisiac and symbol of fertility.

Where found: Worldwide.
Obtainable from: Food shops.
How to use: As a vegetable or as a herb (in powdered form).
Effect: Highly antibacterial, stimulating.

Orchis: Paracelsus first discovered the effect of orchis as an aphrodisiac. He maintained that after eating orchis just once, a man 'could have an erection' 12 times. Probably it was supposed that they had an effect on the male genitals because their knobbly roots resembled testicles. This is backed up by the mention of the orchis root in Greek mythology: Orchis (Greek for testicles) was the son of a nymph and a satyr. When he was killed, he was born again in the form of a beautiful orchid. Satyrs would eat orchis, and the mythical creatures, which were half ram and half human, would become so lusty that they would apparently spray sperm onto the floor!

Orchis was harvested for magical rituals and served with drinks and food. The Indians also considered the bulbs useful for increasing sperm production.

Where found: Europe and the Orient.
Obtainable from: Specialist garden centres.
Note: In many countries, orchis is a protected species.
How to use: The powdered roots can be used as a flour.
Effect: Strengthening.

Parsley: Since olden days, parsley has been widely used as a herb, the root being a medicinal aid. In ancient times the plant was considered a symbol of reincarnation; rumour had it that the plant was capable of creating new life. In the Middle Ages the stalk was used to make lover's magic; the roots were mixed with an enticing cream, and applied to produce ecstasy. The roots and seeds contain an essential oil, with the main ingredient being apiol.

Where found: Cultivated worldwide.

Obtainable from: Food shops, and can be grown in one's garden.

How to use: As a seasoning or as a drink (oil and root extract).

Important note: High doses can lead to abortion.

Effect: Stimulating, slightly enlivening, diuretic. Parsley enhances one's moods, and in high doses is a strong sexual stimulant.

Pepper: For the Indians, pepper is the 'king of herbs'. It was used thousands of years before our time and later brought to Europe by Alexander the Great. Pepper has influenced cultural history and, in its name, battles have been fought and human lives lost. The most famous of all herbs is considered in Asia and Europe to be an aphrodisiac, encouraging sexual intercourse, although higher doses can irritate the mucous membranes.

For a long time those from Arabia ruled the herbal market and brought new recipes for 'kindling sexual lust' to the West. Some herbs were as expensive as gold. False samples – in particular of pepper, saffron and nutmeg – got so out of hand and were considered so socially dangerous that, in the Holy Roman Empire, cheating in spice dealing was punishable by death until 1440.

The standard mixture, which can be sprinkled without thought over just about every meal, and 'does not allow the fire of love ever to go out', was recommended by the Jewish-Arab doctor Moses Maimonides (1135–1204). His recipe was 1 ounce of long pepper, 1 ounce of galangal root, 2 ounces of

cinnamon, 2 ounces of aniseed, $^1/_2$ ounce of mace and $^1/_2$ ounce of nutmeg (1oz = 25g).
Where found: Southern Asia.
Obtainable from: Food shops, and special herbal mixtures from specialist herbalists and head shops.
How to use: As a herb or spice.
Effect: Stimulates, encourages circulation.

Pimento: Traditional Native American medicine uses the fruit and leaves of the pimento tree to treat neuralgia, digestive problems and for warming the body. It kindles sexual lust and is a popular addition to cocoa.
Where found: Central America, Caribbean.
Obtainable from: Delicatessens and food shops.
How to use: As a herb.
Effect: Stimulating.

Pineapple: This tropical fruit contains an enzyme called bromelin, which encourages the digestion of protein. Additionally, pineapples are rich in vitamin C and minerals. It is considered to be an aphrodisiac when eaten with the unlikely accompaniment of chilli powder or when soaked in rum with honey; a small measure a day is said to increase potency.
Where found: South America.
Obtainable from: Food stores.
How to use: As fresh fruit or as juice.
Important note: Unripe fruit can cause miscarriage.
Effect: Strengthening, diuretic, rids one of poisons.

Pomegranate: Throughout Europe and Asia, the pomegranate is a symbol of vitality and immortality. It was valued as a lover's gift. Adam and Eve ate from the Tree of Knowledge, and became aware of their nakedness and the difference between good and evil, which led to the door of Paradise being slammed in their faces. The tree is commonly described as being an apple tree, but because of the supposed location of Eden, it is more likely that the Tree of Knowledge was a pomegranate tree. The fruit was considered in olden days to be an 'apple of love' and was dedicated to Aphrodite as well as Zeus's wife, Hera. The tree stood as a symbol of godly unification with man and the consumption of the fruit and seeds were correspondingly effective. The brilliant red fruit with its many seeds symbolises, like figs, the womb and fertility.

In his book of herbs of 1562, the Italian doctor and man of letters, Matthiolus, recommended: 'For a medicine of some delicacy against the bad ailments and orifices of the secret places of men and women, take the rind of a pomegranate and a sponge, dry out both and grind to powder, and sprinkle on the problem.'

Where found: Asia Minor.

Obtainable from: Supermarkets and delicatessens.

How to use: As a fruit or juice (grenadine).

Effect: Energy giving.

Poppy seeds: The poppy is a plant that has been cultivated since the dawning of human history. Opium was extracted from the sap of the seed pods of the opium poppy, and was considered to be a plant blessed by the gods (the Greek word *opus* means juice). From the poppy, some of the oldest medicines, analgesics and aphrodisiacs have been produced. The poppy contains a complex mixture of alkaloids, the most well known being morphine. Other poppy-derived alkaloids such as codeine, thebaine, papaverine and narcotine play an important role in the narcotic effects of opium.

The healing powers of the sap have been known for 4,500 years. Where this plant originated is unclear but one of the ancient centres for growing and producing opium was Cyprus, the Island of Aphrodite. According to Theocrat, the intoxicating opium juice came from the tears of the Goddess of Love, as she cried for the loss of her loved one, Adonis. Other Greek gods were also associated with the poppy seed: Hypnos, the God of Sleep; his son Morpheus, the provider of dreams, and Dionysos, the God of Intoxication. Nyx, the Goddess of the Night and Ruler of Space was given a string of powers.

Just before the pod fully ripens, it is slit. This always takes place in the evening, so that the milky residue can seep out and dry overnight, to be collected the following morning.

Though illegal, opium is either smoked or eaten. Different cultures use different additives in order to get optimal results and to reduce the side effects, including several nightshade plants, herbs, wine and other types of alcohol. As a stimulant, opium is only effective in small doses, as Krünitz wrote in 1805: 'Another result of blood mobilised by opium is an awakened and increased lust for sexual intercourse that is so great that even old men feel the effect; and the penises of slaughtered Turks in battle were still erect: also the nightly escape of sperm was common with the lusty thoughts. However, too great a loss made men incapable of intercourse.'

The Arabs were probably the first to discover the powers of the 'pleasure plant'. They brought it to Greece, India and China. In order that opium could produce colourful, erotic dreams, it was mixed with special fermented opium (Chinese

Tschandu) before being smoked. Pressed into the shape of little fish the mixture was sold in the markets. The fish symbolises fertility and life in Chinese tradition, but it also represented, as in Italy, the penis. The saying 'fish and water come together' refers to sexual intercourse. Some historians maintain that the fertility of the Chinese people is a result of their consumption of opium.

Where found: Worldwide.

Obtainable from: Some shops will sell opium poppy seeds. Normal red poppy seeds are widely available, although their effect is much weaker.

Note: Growing opium poppy seeds is illegal. Taking opium and its derivatives is illegal without a prescription.

How to use: Smoke, chew or snort (powder).

Effect: Intoxicating, sexually stimulating.

Pumpkin: Pumpkin seeds are highly valued in India as an aphrodisiac, and they play a significant role in certain Tantric love rituals. It is said that if a woman eats pumpkin or melon seeds, she is showing her willingness for sex. The flowers and flesh of the pumpkin are also thought to have aphrodisiac qualities.

Where found: Worldwide.

Obtainable from: Food shops.

How to use: As fruit, or a snack (seeds).

Rosemary: Rosemary has been used dried as incense as well as a seasoning for wine. This evergreen plant was considered to be a plant of death as well as love, which further highlights the association between orgasm and death. Traditionally, brides wore a wreath made from rosemary. Shakespeare's Ophelia also knew about its deep symbolic value: 'And there is rosemary, which stands for faithfulness.' The rosemary that is found in northern Eurasia (Ledum palustre) was used by shamans as a magical herb.

Where found: Eurasia, North Africa, cultivated worldwide.
Obtainable from: Food shops and can be grown in one's garden.
How to use: As a herb.
Important note: In high doses rosemary can cause miscarriage.
Effect: Stimulates circulation, encourages digestion. A bath with rosemary essential oil stimulates, and encourages blood to flow through the skin, so increasing sensitivity.

Saffron: The Greeks believed that saffron aroused female lust. In Islamic medicine, the male pistils of the crocus flower are dried, and the resulting spice is considered to have 'heating' qualities, supposedly increasing the sexual desire of young men and strengthening the female uterus. Because the plant contains essential oils with psychologically activating and stimulating substances, it also became a substitute for opium. Weight-for-weight it is more valuable than gold.

Where found: Asia Minor and North Africa.
Obtainable from: Food shops.
How to use: As a herb.
Important note: High doses of saffron can result in toxic poisoning and can cause miscarriages.
Effect: Stimulating and intoxicating. Intense and long orgasms can result.

Sunflowers: Sunflowers have been cultivated in gardens in Europe since the 16th century, for their beauty as well as their healing powers and nutritional properties. The leaves as well as the flower petals are considered a healing agent for

rheumatism and stomach and bowel ailments. The Mayas boiled the flower petals and drank the tea because of its stimulating effect, caused by the presence of chlorogen acids.
Where found: Worldwide.
Obtainable from: One's garden, or as seeds from health shops.
How to use: As a flour, as a snack (seeds), as tea (petals), as oil.
Effect: Stimulating.

Tea: As with coffee or cocoa, tea is commonly drunk for enjoyment throughout the world. Taoists drank it as a popular stimulant as well as for meditation. Combined with other ingredients such as herbs, wine, ginseng or opium, tea was also considered an aphrodisiac. Paradoxically, the shorter the brewing time, the more stimulating the effect is.
Where found: Asia.
Obtainable from: Tea and food shops, fresh from Asian shops.
How to use: Brew in hot water.
Effect: Stimulating.

Truffles: These mushrooms are the rarest and most sensual of fungi. Colette, the French author, wrote: 'Its magnificent taste will solve all difficulties and problems.'
Where found: Truffles grow underground in the shade of oak trees in the Dordogne, Alsace, Provence, Italy and North Africa.
Obtainable from: Fresh or preserved in delicatessens.
How to use: As a vegetable.
Effect: Stimulating and sensitising.

Vanilla: The scent and flavour of vanilla are said to increase lust, especially when combined with cocoa or arrowroot. The etymology of the word 'vanilla' comes from the same stem as 'vagina' and homoeopathic doctors prescribe vanilla as a cure for impotence all over the world.

Where found: Central America.

Obtainable from: Food shops.

How to use: As a tincture or herb.

Effect: Stimulating and energy-giving.

Vermouth: This is one of the oldest healing plants for gynaecological complaints and in olden days the vermouth plant was dedicated to the young Goddess Artemis. Its branches were used in love potions and the dried leaves were smoked as a substitute for marijuana. Absinthe, brandy made from vermouth and flavoured with aniseed and fennel, became the notorious drug of the bohemians in the 19th century. The leaves of the plant contain the psychedelic, stimulating substance called thujon, which can also be toxic.

Where found: Eurasia, North Africa, America.

Obtainable from: One's garden, dried in specialist herbal shops and in chemists.

How to use: As absinthe or smoked (leaves).

Effect: Slightly psychedelic.

Wine: Wine, along with other forms of alcohol, is without doubt the world's most important and widely used drug. Enjoyment is often for ritual purposes, to experience ecstasy. Wine has been said to be a wonderful aphrodisiac and holy drink since olden times. Cleopatra used it, mixed with raw opium and various nightshade plants, to achieve total lack of inhibitions.

Grapes were cultivated over 5,000 years ago in Mesopotamia. The cult surrounding the intoxicating liquid reached its peak in Greece. To honour the God Dionysus, mass orgies were held, where wine flowed in rivers. However, the holy wine was not drunk pure by Dionysus' followers: vermouth, hyssop, thyme, laurel, myrrh, crocus and marjoram oils, mint, juniper, pepper, henbane, thorn apple, hellebore and opium raised the level of intoxication. It was so strong that the wine had to be well diluted with water, otherwise revellers would have gone mad and remained so.

Where found: Worldwide.

Obtainable from: Off-licences, food shops and wine shops.

How to use: As wine.

Effect: Intoxicating, relaxing.

FOREPLAY

Ａll recipes are of course for two people, unless otherwise stated.

They are dining at their favourite restaurant. A French restaurant, with white tablecloths, folded linen napkins, lots of silver, crystal, chandeliers, high ceilings, and flowers everywhere. It is the ultimate luxury. The thief interrupts his verbose soliloquy with a relishing and satisfying burp. Georgina fills the pause with a soft voice: 'Gourmets don't burp.'

A man sits at the neighbouring table, completely immersed in a book. Eats as if by the way, and does not register the food falling from his fork. Georgina watches him in an amused way. She sees him guiding the empty fork to his open lips. Only when the metal touches his mouth does he look up and meets her quiet smile. They look at each other, judging, curiously touching each other with glances.

The thief speaks: 'Money is my business, and eating my pleasure. Georgina is also my pleasure. Of course on a much more private level.' Laughs loudly and gropes for her under the table.

'One must stuff one's mouth to fill the lavatory bowl. Though these pleasures belong together. As the arousing parts and the dirty parts of the body are placed so closely together one can see how sex and eating belong together.'

Georgina's glances wander repeatedly to the other table. Unexpectedly she gets up and hurries to the toilets. She does not stay long. He had followed her. He shows himself, and his interest, but leaves the room again quickly. Georgina turns round and about – a ballet of indecision. She hurries back to the dining room.

Glances of desire shuttle from table to table. She hurries again to the toilet. 'I forgot my cigarette lighter.' Blushing, she meets him, shyly takes his hand and guides him demandingly to her breasts. The lover urges her into the pale white of the toilets and against a cubicle, starts to undress her. He discovers her black camisole and immaculate alabaster skin. He peppers her with greedy kisses, panting with lust.

Scene from the film *The Cook, The Thief, His Wife and Her Lover*, directed by Peter Greenaway.

A selection of fresh herbs will make any salad special, but lovage is a herb you can trust every time for its aphrodisiac effect.

Spring-in-your-step Salad

mixed salad leaves (choose from iceberg lettuce, curly endive, rocket, lollo rosso, dandelion and young stinging nettles)
6 baby radishes
1 tbs red wine vinegar
3 tbs sunflower oil
salt and freshly ground black pepper
$^1/_2$ clove garlic, crushed
fresh aromatic herbs (chervil, parsley, oregano, lovage), coarsely chopped
to garnish: chives and cress

Wash and dry the salad leaves. Starting from the centre of the top of each radish, cut shallow 'zigzagging' patterns in concentric circles. Place the radishes in a bowl of tepid water so that they open up into little roses. Prepare the dressing by combining the vinegar, oil, salt, pepper, garlic and chopped herbs. Toss the salad leaves and divide them between two serving plates, drizzle the dressing over the salad and sprinkle with chives and cress. Garnish with the radish 'roses'.

Courgette (zucchini) flowers are the ultimate erotic delicacy because they are so delicate. This is a gem of a recipe from Italy.

Frisky Fried Courgette Flowers

3 tbs flour
1 tbs white wine
5 tbs ice cold water + extra for dipping
salt
10 courgette (zucchini) or pumpkin flowers
peanut oil for deep frying

Mix the flour, wine and water together, and add some salt. Let the batter stand for around 30 minutes. Very carefully dip the flowers in cold water, holding them upside down by the stems. Leave them on kitchen paper until they have completely dried. When dry, lightly press them together so that they do not take on too much batter. Hold them upside down by the stem and dip in the batter, taking care to shake off any excess. Deep-fry them for around a minute in hot oil. Before serving, lay the flowers on kitchen roll to absorb excess oil.

Variation: You can stuff the flowers before frying. Carefully spoon a mixture consisting of half a finely chopped anchovy fillet and coarsely chopped mozzarella cheese into each flower, then fry.

Because of their shape and their fast growth, in times gone by mushrooms were known as the phalluses of the earth. Truffles and morels are highly thought of by aphrodisiac connoisseurs, but mushrooms definitely play their part as well.

Snugly Stuffed Mushrooms

10 large flat mushrooms
3 shallots
butter for frying
1 bunch parsley
thyme sprigs
salt and freshly ground black pepper
sweet paprika
4 tbs ($^1/_3$ cup) dry white wine

Clean the mushrooms and remove the stems. Very finely dice all the stems, along with two of the mushrooms. Remove the skin of the shallots and chop them finely. Heat 1 tablespoon of butter in a pan and fry the shallots until they are translucent. Add the chopped mushrooms. As the mushrooms fry, add as much butter as they need to absorb. Season the mushrooms with chopped herbs, salt, pepper and paprika and cook over a medium heat, until any moisture has been absorbed. Fill the remaining eight mushroom heads with this mixture, and place in a greased baking tin. Pour the wine over the mushrooms and bake in an oven pre-heated to 200°C (400°F) for 25 minutes. Serve with a salad.

'The roots and flesh of the artichoke, when eaten with salt, pepper opens the way for unchaste deeds.'

P. A. Matthiolus, Italian doctor and
teacher, 16th century.

Quail and Artichoke Salad

2 whole globe artichokes
lemon juice
rocket
2 quails
salt and freshly ground black pepper
butter
2 tbs grape seed oil
1 tbs sherry vinegar

Remove the stems, leaves and surrounding fibres from the artichokes. Bring some water to the boil and add a squeeze of lemon juice. Cut the artichokes into fine strips and blanch them for around a minute in the boiling water. Plunge the strips into cold water and dry them thoroughly with kitchen paper. Wash the rocket and drain well. Mix it with the artichokes.

Next, clean the quails thoroughly and de-bone them: cut the meat from the top of the breastbone down to where the legs join the body. Separate and remove the two halves of breast meat and remove the bone, so that the legs are attached to the de-boned breast. Season the meat with salt and pepper, and fry in hot butter until it is cooked pink, taking care not to overcook the meat. Set aside until the quails cool and then carefully remove the legs from the breast meat.

Shortly before serving, make up a dressing with salt, pepper, oil and vinegar and drizzle it over the artichokes and rocket. Slice each quail breast in two, and serve together with the legs on a bed of the salad.

Some believe that both rabbit and hare meat are aphrodisiacs because of the animals' prolific breeding habits.

Raring-to-go Rabbit Salad

1 rabbit fillet
freshly ground black pepper
3 juniper berries
salt
butter for frying
50 g (2 oz or $^{1}/_{2}$ cup) mushrooms, sliced
2 rashers smoked streaky bacon
$^{1}/_{2}$ tsp honey
1 tbs olive oil
2 tbs apple vinegar
radicchio leaves and lamb's lettuce in equal quantities
chives to garnish

Wash and dry the rabbit fillet. Rub the meat with the black pepper and juniper berries. Fry it for a minute or two to seal it, and then season with salt. Reduce the heat and fry for 10 minutes, turning occasionally. Add the mushrooms a few minutes before the rabbit is done. Remove from the pan and set aside in a warm place.

Finely dice the bacon and fry it in the same butter that was used to cook the rabbit. Remove the bacon from the pan and stir the honey into the cooking juices. Remove from the heat and add the olive oil, vinegar, salt and pepper. Drizzle the dressing over the salad. Slice the rabbit fillet and arrange the slices on the plates, next to or on top of the salad. Garnish with chives and the bacon cubes.

'Asparagus is a favourite dish of the idler, because whenever it is eaten, it weakens the will.'
Adamus Lonicerus in *The Book of Herbs* (1783).

Perky Pork and Asparagus Salad

100 g ($^1/_4$ lb) white asparagus
100 g ($^1/_4$ lb) green asparagus
225 g ($^1/_2$ lb) pork fillet
white pepper
1 tbs vegetable oil
2 tbs balsamic vinegar
3 tbs olive oil
few sprigs of rosemary
2 sprigs of thyme
lemon balm leaves to garnish

Wash and peel the white asparagus and steam in a little salt water for 15–18 minutes. Peel the lower third of the green asparagus and steam for up to 10 minutes in salted water. Drain the asparagus.

Wash the pork, dab it dry with kitchen paper and coat it in pepper. Fry for a minute or two on a very high heat to seal it, and then reduce the heat and fry for 7–9 minutes – the meat should still be pink on the inside.

While the pork is frying, put the vinegar, olive oil, rosemary and thyme leaves in a separate saucepan and heat slowly, stirring constantly.

Cut the pork into very thin slices and dip both sides into the warm marinade. Serve with both kinds of asparagus and garnish the meat with lemon balm leaves.

Oysters are widely believed to be the strongest aphrodisiac, perhaps because of their texture, but more likely because of their zinc content, which is vital for a healthy reproductive system and male potency. In the past, sometimes even the powdered shell was used in love potions. King Ludwig IV is said to have presented his Spanish wife, the Infanta Maria Theresa, with 400 oysters on their wedding day.

Orgasmic Oysters on Leaf Spinach with Champagne Sauce

12 oysters
200 g (7 oz) fresh leaf spinach
2 shallots
50 g (2 oz or half a stick) butter
125 ml (½ cup) single (light) cream
7 tbs (½ cup) champagne
salt and freshly ground white pepper
pinch grated nutmeg
cayenne pepper to taste
1 tsp lemon juice
1 tsp chives, finely chopped

Carefully open the oysters using an oyster knife and prise the flesh from the shells, taking care to reserve all the juice from the oysters. Wash the spinach, blanch in boiling water for a few seconds and then plunge into cold water so that the leaves keep their colour. Finely chop one of the shallots and fry it in butter until it is translucent, making sure that it does not brown. Add the spinach and fry for a few moments.

For the sauce, finely chop the remaining shallot, and fry it in 1 tablespoon of butter until it is translucent. Add the cream and cook on a high heat until the sauce has reduced and thickened. Add the champagne and cook for a minute or so. Season with salt, pepper, nutmeg, cayenne pepper and lemon juice. Remove the sauce from the heat and add the oyster juices, which should be sieved to remove sand or shell fragments.

Real oyster fans and would-be lovers should eat the oysters raw, but if preferred, the oysters can be placed in the hot sauce for up to 20 seconds to lightly cook them, and removed using a slotted spoon. Arrange the spinach on two plates, and lay the oysters on it. Stir the sauce and add cubes of the remaining butter, allowing them to melt. Pour the sauce over the oysters and garnish with chives.

Variation: As there is a lot of sauce, it can be served in four of the oyster shells (two on each plate) instead of being poured on top of the oysters.

Aphrodite rose out of the sea in a sea shell, off the coast of Cyprus. In many cultures, mussels and other shellfish are seen as a symbol of the vulva, and from ancient to modern times, mussels have been believed to kindle and arouse lovers' ardour.

Mouth-watering Mussels in Riesling Sauce

1 kg (2 lbs) mussels
1 carrot
1 stick celery
$^1/_3$ leek (white part only)
1 clove garlic
1 shallot
2 tbs olive oil
salt and freshly ground pepper
125 ml ($^1/_2$ cup) Riesling wine
$^1/_2$ bunch flat leaf parsley
crusty baguette

Carefully sort the mussels. Wash them under running water and remove their 'beards'. Discard any open ones. Finely chop the carrot, celery, leek, garlic and shallot. Heat the oil in a saucepan and fry the garlic and shallot until they are translucent. Add the vegetables, salt and pepper and sweat them for a few minutes. Add the wine and mussels and cook in a covered saucepan for 4–5 minutes, regularly shaking the pot. The mussels are ready when the shells are open. Discard any shells that have not opened. Garnish the mussels with chopped parsley and serve in deep bowls with a baguette.

Ginger is renowned in many parts of the world for its ability
to arouse sexual passion.

Spicy Goose Breast with Melons and Fresh Ginger

$2^1/_2$ cm (1 in) ginger root
$^1/_2$ canteloupe melon
100 g ($^1/_3$ lb) smoked goose breast
mint leaves to garnish

Remove the skin of the ginger and cut into thin straws.
Blanch for a minute in hot, salted water. Remove from
the water and leave to cool on kitchen paper. Remove the
seeds and rind from the melon and cut into thin, large slices.
Arrange in a fan on the plate and top with the ginger. Cut the
goose into thin slices, and serve alongside the melon. Garnish
with mint leaves.

'The avocado arouses sexual passion. Ludwig IV called it *la bonne poire* (the good pear) because it appeared to revive his declining libido.'
Robert Hendrikson in *Fools for Love* (1974).

Avocado, Mussel and Caviar Salad

2 shallots
2 tbs olive oil
juice of 2 lemons
$^1/_2$ tbs fresh basil, chopped
6–8 green peppercorns, slightly crushed
4 large green-lipped mussels
2 avocados
salt and freshly ground black pepper
2 tsp salmon or trout caviar
1 tbs chives, finely chopped

Finely chop the shallots and mix them with the olive oil, three-quarters of the lemon juice, basil and peppercorns. Wash the mussels, and finely chop the white part, leaving the pink parts intact. Marinate the mussels in the dressing, and cool in the fridge for one hour. Halve the avocados lengthways and remove the stones. Squeeze a little lemon juice over the flesh to prevent it from browning. Carefully remove the avocado from its skin, taking care to keep the skin in one piece. Keep two of the skins for serving. Purée the avocado with the rest of the lemon juice. Season with salt and black pepper.

Remove the mussels from the marinade, and keeping back two of the pink parts of the mussels for the garnish, mix them into the avocado purée.

Spoon the mixture into the avocado shells and garnish each one with a pink part of the mussel, the caviar and chives.

Apples and nuts are traditional symbols of female fertility, and it is said that celery works wonders for male potency.

Come-to-the-crunch Celery Salad

200 g (1 or 2 medium) cooking apples
head of baby celery
lemon juice
50 g (scant $^1/_2$ cup) walnuts, chopped
3 tbs whipped cream
salt and freshly ground white pepper
pinch sugar
3 tbs mayonnaise
salad leaves, cress, walnut kernels, baby tomatoes to garnish

Peel the apples and peel the strands off the sticks of celery. Cut them both into pieces approximately $2^1/_2$ cm (1 inch) long. Squeeze lemon juice over the apple straight away to prevent it from going brown. Add the walnuts to the apple and celery.

For the dressing, combine the whipped cream, salt, pepper and a pinch of sugar with the mayonnaise. Stir the salad into the dressing and leave in the fridge to cool. Before serving, decorate with salad leaves, cress, walnuts and tomatoes.

Core, the daughter of Demeter, was kidnapped by Hades and taken down into the depths of the earth, where she was fed pomegranate seeds. These seeds transformed her from an innocent girl into both a woman and a lover, and when she emerged, she took the new name of Persephone.

Persephone's Liver Salad with Pomegranate Vinaigrette

1 tbs raisins

2–3 tbs red wine

1 pomegranate

1 tbs capers

1 tsp balsamic vinegar

1 tsp red wine vinegar

salt and freshly ground pepper

1 tsp liquid honey

1 tbs olive oil

3 tbs vegetable oil

$1/3$ head iceberg lettuce

100 g ($1/4$ lb) fresh duck liver

2 tbs strong meat stock

Soak the raisins in the wine and leave covered for a couple of hours to allow them to absorb the wine. Halve the pomegranate diagonally and remove the seeds. Add the seeds and capers to the soaked raisins and mix well.

Mix a salad dressing with the two vinegars, salt, pepper, honey, olive oil and two tablespoons of vegetable oil and add to the pomegranate mixture. Wash and dry the lettuce, and break into bite-sized pieces.

Clean and dice the liver, removing any fat and sinews. Heat the rest of the vegetable oil and fry the liver over a very high heat for about a minute to seal in the juices. Remove from the heat and keep the liver warm.

Add the concentrated stock to the pan and reduce the liquid to half the original volume. Moisten the liver in these juices before serving.

Toss the lettuce and dressing together in a basin to form a salad, share the salad between the two plates and arrange the liver on top of the salad. Pour any remaining juices from the pan over the liver before serving.

Figs are the crowning glory of any romantic meal, and this simple dish is no exception.

Beguiling Honeydew Melon, Parma Ham and Figs

2 small honeydew melons
8 ripe figs
150 g (5 oz) Parma ham

Make sure that the melons are well chilled. Halve each melon and carefully remove the seeds, then cut lengthways into slices and remove the skin. Arrange eight slices on each plate in a star formation. Remove the skin from the figs, place them in alternate spaces between the melon slices, and finally arrange the ham in the remaining spaces on the plate.

The throes of passion can make you cry, and it is exactly the same with onions. Onions are known to arouse passion – some religions, such as the Hare Krishna sect of Hinduism, forbid onions in the diet for this reason. When combined with stimulating cloves and strengthening ginger, onions are a foolproof food.

Greek-style Onions

2 medium-sized onions
8 cloves
2 tbs olive oil
$^1/_2$ tsp sugar
$^3/_4$ glass red wine
juice of half a lemon
$^1/_2$ tsp ground ginger
1 tsp capers
salt and freshly ground black pepper

Remove the skin from the onions and stick four cloves in each one. Fry them in hot oil and sugar until they are golden brown, turning them often. Add the wine, lemon juice, ginger and capers and season with salt and pepper. Cook over a low heat for 15 minutes and serve with a salad.

Shrimp and spices can turn any night into a wedding night!

Ceylonese Wedding Cakes

300 g (1 cup) yellow lentils
150 g (1 cup) finely chopped onions
225 g (½ lb) shrimp
80 g (½ cup) soaked raisins
3 tbs finely chopped red chillies
2 tbs chopped almonds
3 tbs flour
1 tsp salt
1 tsp garam masala
pinch cinnamon
pinch saffron
½ tsp ginger
½ tsp chilli powder
oil for frying

Soak the lentils overnight, mash them slightly and cook until they have turned into a mushy purée. Sweat the onions. Remove from the heat and add the shrimp, raisins, chillies, almonds, flour and lentils. Mix well and season with salt and the spices. Mould the mixture into four patties and fry in hot oil until both sides are golden brown.

SINFUL SOUPS

'Those who have thoughts of producing children, with the delight and pleasure that accompanies the act, will require more semen. Their coitus will be more effective, if they, before they commence this business, prepare a vegetable soup with fresh bread and half raw egg white, so that it becomes milky. Before he takes a woman, he should eat this for three or four days each morning and evening before the meal. I don't believe there is anything better in this case.'

D. Agostino Lamponani, from
Abate Cassinese, 1653.

The witches of Thessaloniki and the wise women of
India used to prescribe asparagus juice as a love potion.
The Italian doctor, P. A. Matthiolus, wrote: 'When asparagus
is included in the diet, it causes men to have lustful longings
and desires.'

Asparagus Soup

225 g (¹/₂ lb) white asparagus (it does not have to be the
best quality)
50 g (2 oz or ¹/₂ a stick) butter
5–6 tbs (scant ¹/₂ cup) single (light) cream
5–6 tbs veal or chicken stock
salt and freshly ground black pepper
1 tbs whipped cream
chervil leaves to garnish

Wash and peel the asparagus. Cut the heads off and chop
the stalks into pieces about 2–3 centimetres (1 inch)
long. Heat some butter and cook the asparagus for 8–10
minutes. Remove the heads and put to one side. Add the
cream and meat stock to the rest of the asparagus and cook
for a few minutes. Purée finely in a mixer and season with salt
and pepper. Before serving, stir in the whipped cream; arrange
the asparagus heads and the chervil leaves on top of the soup.

Merry Mussel Soup

225 g (¹/₂ lb) black mussels
1 small onion
25 g (1 oz or ¹/₂ stick) butter
250 ml (1 cup) dry white wine
330 ml (1¹/₂ cups) chicken or vegetable stock
salt and freshly ground black pepper
250 ml (1 cup) sour cream
6 green-lipped mussels (or 12 mussels if not available)
1 tsp lemon juice
pinch grated nutmeg
1 egg yolk
1 bunch parsley
1 sprig thyme

Clean and finely chop the black mussels and blanch them for a few seconds in boiling water. Finely chop the onion and sweat in hot butter. Add the mussels and cook for 5 minutes. Next add the wine and stock, season with salt and pepper and simmer for 20 minutes. Pass the soup through a fine sieve and add the sour cream.

While the soup is cooking, take the green-lipped mussels and fry them in some butter and lemon juice for 10 minutes. Season with a pinch of nutmeg, salt and pepper.

Bring the soup back to the boil and then remove it from the stove and stir in the egg yolk. Before serving, put half the green-lipped mussels into each bowl, sprinkle with chopped parsley and thyme, ladle the soup over them and serve immediately.

The Egyptians believed that the onion was an aphrodisiac as far back as 3500 BC. In the Middle Ages, monks were forbidden to eat onions lest they gave in to temptation.

Aphrodisiac Onion Soup

2 medium-sized onions
1 tbs butter
salt and freshly ground black pepper
$^1/_2$ tsp mixed herbs (thyme, rosemary, tarragon, oregano, marjoram)
pinch of ground caraway seeds
1 tbs flour
350 ml (1$^1/_2$ cups) meat stock
150 ml (generous $^1/_2$ cup) white wine
2 pieces white bread
50 g ($^1/_2$ cup) grated gruyère or emmental cheese

Slice the onions into thin rings and fry in butter until they are golden brown. Season the onions with salt, pepper, herbs and a pinch of caraway. Sieve the flour over the onions. Sweat the ingredients briefly and add the stock while stirring constantly so that flour lumps do not form. Add the wine and cook the soup over a low heat for 15 minutes.

Toast the bread under the grill, and then spread the cheese on the top of each slice. Place the bread in fireproof soup bowls, and carefully pour the soup over it – the bread should float at the top of the soup. Place the bowls under the grill until the cheese has melted, and serve immediately.

According to the ancient Greeks, saffron stimulated female desire, and hastened the sexual development of young men. As the most expensive spice in the world, saffron has an exotic and luxurious reputation.

Saffron Fish Soup

225 g ($^1/_2$ lb) white fish fillets
1 small kohlrabi
1 small leek
1 shallot, diced
1 clove garlic, finely chopped
25 g (1 oz or $^1/_3$ stick) butter
1 tbs flour
500 ml (2 cups) fish stock
large pinch saffron
salt and freshly ground white pepper
squeeze of lemon juice
2 tbs double (heavy) cream
1 tsp chives, finely chopped

Wash the fish in cold water and cut into bite-sized strips. Peel the kohlrabi and cut into thin narrow strips, and finely slice the leek. Fry the shallot with the garlic in the butter until the shallot is translucent. Add the vegetables and flour and sweat for a few minutes, stirring often. Pour the stock into the pan while stirring with a wooden spoon, so the flour doesn't form lumps. Season with a good pinch of saffron, salt and pepper. Cook on a low heat for 6–8 minutes. Season the fish pieces with salt and pepper and lemon juice, and place them in the soup stock. Cook for around 2 minutes and then remove the fish, placing it in the two soup bowls. Stir in the double cream, briefly bring to the boil and pour the soup over the fish. Garnish with chives before serving.

This is not a recipe for a chaste evening.

Sweet, Hot and Sour Fish Soup

225 g ($^1/_2$ lb) fish fillets (preferably sole and tuna)
4 tomatoes
2 onions
1 leek
2 sticks celery
2 slices fresh pineapple
2 tbs lemon juice or wine vinegar
125 g (2 cups) fresh beansprouts
salt and freshly ground black pepper
1 tsp sugar
1 tsp oil
2 tbs Vietnamese fish sauce (nuoc mam)
1 fresh red chilli, finely chopped
fresh basil to garnish

Wash and dice the fish fillets. Boil the tomatoes whole, remove their skins and then quarter them. Thinly slice the onions and chop the leek and celery into 2–3 centimetre (1 inch) pieces. Bring half a litre of water to the boil. Add the onions, tomatoes, leek, pineapple and lemon juice or vinegar and cook for 10 minutes. Next, add the fish, beansprouts, salt, pepper, sugar, oil, fish sauce and the chopped chilli and cook for 5 minutes. Garnish with finely chopped basil and serve immediately.

'Aniseed, ginger and coriander will succeed where other
remedies have failed.'
Jacobus Theodorus Tabernaemontanus in
The New and Comprehensive Herb Book, 1731.

Geisha Soup

60 g (2 oz) pork fillet
$^1/_2$ tsp rice or wheat flour
1 tsp ground coriander (cilantro) seeds
pinch sugar
freshly ground black pepper
225 g ($^1/_2$ lb) pak choy or other Chinese greens
1 tbs butter
1 tsp fresh ginger, finely chopped
salt
1 egg
pinch star anise
500 ml (2 cups) water

Cut the pork into wafer-thin strips. Mix the flour,
coriander, a pinch of sugar, salt and pepper and coat the
strips of meat in the mixture. Chop the pak choy into pieces
about 2 centimetres (1 inch) thick.

Heat the butter in a saucepan and fry the ginger and salt for
half a minute. Add the pak choy, and immediately pour the
water into the pot and cook over a low heat for 5 minutes.
Whisk the egg together with the star anise, remove the soup
from the heat and stir in the egg until it sets. Serve
immediately.

'He who loves crabs is bound to be pinched by love.'

Danish saying.

Catch–me Crab Soup

1 onion
500 ml (2 cups) chicken broth
1 lobster stock cube (a fish stock cube will do)
225 g ($^1/_2$ lb) fresh, uncooked crab meat (not including shell)
2 tbs crème fraîche or soured cream
salt and freshly ground pepper
fresh dill or parsley to garnish

Finely chop the onion and place in a saucepan with the broth. Bring to a rolling boil and add the stock cube. As soon as it has dissolved, reduce the heat, so that the soup simmers for 10 minutes. Remove from the heat and add the crab meat and crème fraîche, stirring well, and leave to stand for 10 minutes. Season with salt and pepper. If you must reheat the soup before serving, do not let it boil – or even come close to boiling. Before serving, garnish with chopped dill or parsley.

'Without lemons, love would not blossom.'
Hugo Hertwig, German biologist, in *Healing Plants*, 1964.

Luscious Lemon Soup

4 garlic cloves
2 tbs olive oil
30 g (1 oz) uncooked rice
500 ml (2 cups) vegetable stock
freshly ground black pepper
1 clove
1 tbs grated lemon peel
15 mint leaves, finely chopped
3 egg yolks
juice of half a lemon
salt

Finely chop the garlic and fry in hot oil, taking care that it does not brown. Add the rice and fry for 2–3 minutes, stirring constantly, so that the rice does not stick. Add the vegetable stock, pepper and clove, and simmer on a low heat for 40 minutes. Five minutes before the cooking time is up, add the lemon peel and mint leaves. Take the soup from the stove and remove the clove. In a large basin, beat the egg yolks thoroughly, and mix with the lemon juice. Pour the egg yolk mixture into the hot soup, stirring constantly – the egg yolk must not set or curdle. Season with salt before serving.

Exotic spices don't just make a meal more tasty, they also
stimulate the libido.

Mulligatawny Meat Soup

300 g (8 oz) ground lean beef mince
2 medium onions, finely chopped
1 tbs butter
1 red chilli pepper
1 tsp coriander (cilantro) seeds
pinch of ground caraway
freshly ground black pepper
1 tbs curry powder
pinch of sugar
salt
3 cloves garlic
1 small tin tomato purée
375 ml (1¹/₂ cups) water
fresh coriander (cilantro) leaves

Fry the beef and onions in half the butter. While they are
cooking, finely chop the chilli pepper and lightly grind the
coriander seeds in a mortar and pestle. Carefully fry the chilli,
coriander, caraway, black pepper, curry powder, sugar and salt
in a separate pan with the rest of the butter, taking care that it
does not burn. Add the cooked spices to the beef and cook for
another couple of minutes, then add the garlic. Next add the
tomato purée and the water, and simmer on a low heat for 30
minutes. Serve garnished with coriander leaves.

Regarding chilli: 'One should never add more than 12 seeds to a dish, otherwise one will cause suffering, and people will be driven quite mad.'

Adamus Lonicerus in *The Herb Book* (1783).

Pumpin' Pumpkin Soup

2 cloves garlic
1 red chilli pepper
500 ml (2 cups) meat stock
2–3 tbs peanut (groundnut) oil
1 medium onion, chopped
2 slices toast
225 g (1/2 lb) pumpkin, finely chopped
salt
80 g (3 oz) fresh leaf spinach

Using a pestle and mortar, grind the garlic and chilli into a paste (you can use more than 12 seeds, as 'erotic madness' is after all the aim of this dish!). Empty the garlic and chilli into a saucepan and add the meat stock while stirring constantly over a low heat, bringing the mixture to a slow boil. In another saucepan, heat the oil and fry the onion until it is golden brown. Remove the crusts from the toast and fry the bread in the onion and oil mixture until golden, then pour in the meat stock. Add the pumpkin to the soup and simmer for around 10 minutes. Season with salt, and then liquidise the soup in a blender. Pour it back into the saucepan and re-heat, add the leaf spinach and then simmer on a low heat for 5 minutes before serving.

A shot of vermouth inspires ardour. This recipe is an energising idea from the Far East.

Naughty Nori Soup with Egg

2 large sheets nori seaweed
500 ml (2 cups) chicken stock
2 spring onions (scallions), finely chopped
$^1/_3$ tsp ginger, finely chopped
1 tbs vermouth
dash of sesame oil
salt and freshly ground pepper
2 eggs

Roast the nori sheets very briefly in a dry pan, until they turn a greenish colour. Crumble the sheets and add to the chicken stock. Bring the stock to the boil and then reduce the heat, and add all the ingredients except for the eggs. Whisk the eggs and pour into the soup. As soon as the soup has thickened, remove from the heat and serve immediately.

This delicious soup can be served warm or chilled.

Cool Courgette Soup

2 medium-sized courgettes (zucchini)
2 medium-sized onions
500 ml (2 cups) chicken or vegetable stock
125 ml (¹/₂ cup) natural yogurt
salt and freshly ground black pepper
chives to garnish

Cut the courgettes into sticks and the onions into thick slices. Bring the stock to the boil and add the vegetables. Simmer until the courgettes can easily be pierced with a knife. Liquidise the soup and add the yogurt. Season with salt and pepper and garnish with chives. If the soup is to be served chilled, cool in the refrigerator for a few hours before serving.

OCEANS OF LOVE

'In France, we know that those who live almost exclusively on shellfish and fish, which are mostly made up of water, are much more fiery in love than others. Indeed, we feel much more drawn towards love during Lent than at any other time of the year, not because of required abstinence, but because during this time we sustain ourselves on fish and herbs; nourishments that contain much water.'

Nicolas Venette in *Paper on the Procreation of Humans*, 1762.

Saucy Steamed Fish with Saffron

450 g (1 lb) white freshwater fish
1 tbs fruit vinegar
salt
1 tbs oil for frying
1 medium onion
125 ml (½ cup) water
10 basil leaves, finely chopped

For the marinade:
1 medium onion
2 cloves garlic
1 tsp saffron strands
1 tbs Vietnamese fish sauce (nuoc mam)

For the sauce:
1 clove garlic
freshly ground black pepper
1 red chilli pepper, chopped
1 tsp finely sliced ginger
2 tbs Vietnamese fish sauce (nuoc mam)

Scale, gut and clean the fish thoroughly. Either use whole or cut into 2–3 centimetre (1 inch) thick slices, and rub with vinegar and salt.

For the marinade, chop the onion very finely and crush the cloves of garlic, and combine with the saffron and the fish sauce. Pour over the fish and leave to stand for 2 hours.

While the fish is marinating, make the sauce. Crush the garlic, add the black pepper, chilli, ginger and fish sauce and pour into a sauce-boat. Allow to stand until serving so the fish sauce absorbs the flavour of the seasonings.

When the fish has marinated, heat some oil in a pan and fry a few slices of onion until they are brown but not burnt. Add the water, fish and marinade to the pan. Bring to the boil and then simmer, covered for 30 minutes so that the fish steams. Five minutes before the fish is ready, add half the basil leaves. To serve, place the sauce-boat in the middle of a large plate. Arrange the fish on one side, and the rest of the basil leaves on the other. Serve with steamed rice.

Steaming Catfish

2 large catfish cutlets (or other freshwater fish)
2 tbs lemon or lime juice
salt and freshly ground white pepper
1 tbs ground coriander
150 ml (generous $^1/_2$ cup) fish stock
2 tbs ice-cold butter

Wash the fish steaks and drizzle them with lemon or lime juice. Season with salt, pepper and coriander, and lay in a greased steamer.

In a saucepan, bring the stock to the boil. Place the steamer over the stock and cover. Steam for 2 minutes, then turn the fish and steam for a further 3 minutes. Take the fish out and keep it warm.

Cut the butter into small cubes, and bit by bit whisk it into the stock. Season, and serve with the fish. Serve with steamed broccoli or boiled new potatoes.

Perfect Perch with Orange Sauce

2 perch fillets (or any other freshwater fish)
juice of one lemon
2 tbs flour
50 g (2 oz or $1/2$ a stick) butter
salt and coarsely ground black pepper
juice of one orange

Drizzle the lemon juice over the fish fillets. Leave the fish to marinade in the fridge for one hour. Shake them to remove excess marinade and coat with flour. Fry in hot butter until they are golden brown. Season with salt and a lot of black pepper, and add the orange juice. While they are cooking, baste frequently with the butter in the pan. Serve with boiled new potatoes.

Steamed Salmon in Champagne *Sabayon*

2 large salmon fillets
2 tbs lemon juice
salt and freshly ground white pepper
150 ml (²/₃ cup) fish stock
2 egg yolks
1 tsp cornflour
75 ml (¹/₃ cup) champagne (or white wine)

Carefully remove the bones from the salmon. Squeeze lemon juice over the fish and season with salt and pepper. Lay the salmon in a greased steaming basket, place in a saucepan of water and cover. Steam for 1 minute, turn the fish and steam for a further 3–4 minutes. Take the fish out and keep warm. Gently heat the stock.

Whisk the egg yolks, cornflour, salt and pepper together in a basin, and place in a bain-marie (a saucepan of warm water). Whip the warmed, but not too hot, stock and the champagne into the egg yolk mixture until it is a thick and foamy sauce (a *sabayon*). Season and serve the *sabayon* with the salmon. Serve with a combination of long grain and wild rice.

Skewered King Prawns

10 raw king prawns
2 cloves garlic, crushed
3 tbs olive oil
salt and freshly ground black pepper
1 tsp oregano, finely ground
pinch of cayenne pepper
$^1/_2$ lemon and its rind

Wash and clean the prawns. Using kitchen scissors, cut the entire length of the top of each prawn, and remove the vein and guts. Whisk the garlic together with the oil, salt, pepper, herbs and spices. Mix in the zest of the lemon and some of the lemon juice. Add the prawns and marinate in the fridge for 3–4 hours. Skewer the prawns and grill them for 6 minutes, turning halfway through cooking. Serve with garlic bread.

Trout with Capers and Sage

2 medium-sized trout or other white fish
juice of 1 lemon
2 tbs flour
50 g (2 oz or ½ a stick) butter
4 sage leaves
1 tbs capers
3 tbs white wine

Wash the fish, and dry it thoroughly. Rub salt into it and drizzle most of the lemon juice over. Leave to stand for 1 hour in the fridge.

Once the fish has marinated, dry it using kitchen paper and coat with flour. Heat the butter in a pan and fry the fish with the sage leaves until it is golden brown. Shake the pan occasionally, so that it does not stick. Turn the fish and spread the capers over it. Squeeze more lemon juice onto it and add the wine. Baste with the butter and wine mixture so that it does not dry out while cooking.

Remove the fish from the stove and keep covered for 2 minutes so that the aroma of the capers can fully penetrate it. Serve with new boiled potatoes.

Scrumptious Squid and Vegetables

1 clove garlic
$^1/_2$ bunch parsley
1 stick pepperoni
3 tbs olive oil
100 ml (scant $^1/_2$ cup) red wine
2 large tomatoes
450 g (1 lb) fresh or deep frozen squid
150 g beet leaves (6 oz) (pre-cooked and pressed dry)
salt
squeeze of lemon juice

Crush the garlic and chop the parsley, and mix the two together. Fry half the mixture with the pepperoni in oil, and add the wine. Peel the tomatoes, pierce all over with a fork and add to the pan.

Clean and gut the squid, cut into rings and separate the tentacles. Add them to the pepperoni mixture and cook for 1 hour. About 40 minutes into the cooking time, add the beet leaves and some salt. When the hour is up, add the rest of the garlic and parsley mixture and season with lemon juice. Serve with polenta or bread.

Cupid's Calamari

1 stale bread roll
100 ml (scant $^1/_2$ cup) milk
300 g (10 oz) squid
$^1/_2$ lemon
80 g (3 oz) mortadella ham
1 clove garlic, crushed
1 egg
1 egg yolk
1 bunch parsley, finely chopped
salt and freshly ground pepper
4 tbs olive oil
4 tbs white wine

Break the bread roll into small pieces, and soak in milk. Remove the ink sac and the eyes from the squid and discard. Wash the squid thoroughly. Cook in boiling, salted water, along with slices of lemon for 20 minutes. Finely chop the squid tentacles and the mortadella. Mix the garlic, egg, egg yolk, parsley and the bread roll (squeeze the excess milk out first) and season with salt and pepper. Fill the squid tubes with the stuffing and sew up the opening with cooking thread. Lay the tubes in a greased heat-proof dish and drizzle with oil. Bake in a preheated oven for about 20–30 minutes at 180(C (350(F). Halfway through cooking, add the white wine to make a sauce, which can be poured over the squid before serving. Serve with steamed rice or risotto.

Fillet of Steamed Fish in Green Sauce

1 head celery
1 carrot
1 leek
125 ml ($^1/_2$ cup) full fat cream cheese
1 tbs parsley, chopped
1 tsp tarragon
2 shallots
225 g ($^1/_2$ lb) fresh fish bones or fish heads
450 g (1 lb) white fish fillets
salt and freshly ground black pepper
1 tsp Pernod (or to taste)

Using a potato peeler, remove the fibres from the celery and cut into fine strips. Cut the carrot into strips of a similar size and finely chop the leek. Boil the vegetables. Meanwhile, blend the cream cheese together with the parsley, tarragon and a third of the chopped shallots. Put the fish bones or fish heads, vegetables and the rest of the chopped shallots in a saucepan and cover with 2–3 centimetres (1 inch) of water. Lay the fish fillets in a steamer. Put the steamer in the saucepan, cover and cook for 2–3 minutes.

Put 3 tablespoons of the liquid used to steam the fish in a pan and reduce over a high heat to 1 teaspoon. Add the herb and cream cheese mixture and cook until the sauce has thickened. Season with salt and pepper and add Pernod.

Arrange the fillets on a warmed plate and serve the sauce separately.

Salmon Pasta Indulgence

1 large salmon fillet
1 shallot
butter for frying
200 ml (generous ³/₄ cup) double (heavy) cream
300 g (10 oz) fresh tagliatelle
freshly ground black pepper

Carefully remove the skin and bones from the salmon and cut into bite-sized pieces. Finely chop the shallot and fry in butter until golden brown. Pour in the cream, add the salmon, and cook over a medium heat for about 3–4 minutes.

Meanwhile, cook the tagliatelle until it is 'al dente' (fresh pasta only needs a few minutes), and serve a portion into each bowl. Pour the salmon sauce over the tagliatelle and season with a little freshly ground black pepper before serving.

Cheeky Charr in White Wine Sauce

250 ml (1 cup) white wine
1 carrot, cut into thin strips
1 onion, finely chopped
$1/2$ tsp fresh thyme, chopped
bunch of flat leaf parsley
1 bay leaf
salt
6 black peppercorns
2 whole charr or other small freshwater fish

In a pan, cook the wine, carrot, onion, thyme, most of the parsley, bay leaf, salt and peppercorns for 15 minutes. Remove the sauce from the heat and leave to cool for a couple of minutes. Salt the insides of the fish, and lay the fish in the sauce. Leave covered for 10 minutes. Check to see if the fish is cooked – if it is still raw, give it a couple more minutes. Remove the fish and place on a pre-warmed plate. Serve with the wine sauce and boiled new potatoes.

ANIMAL LUST

For Thomas Aquinas the desire for meat constituted mortal sins of both gluttony and pleasure. Accordingly, many servants of God banned meat from their kitchens altogether. Many gourmets, on the other hand, refused to forego meat. Apart from enjoying the usual cuts of beef, lamb, veal and pork, they would also enjoy bone marrow, and the sexual organs of a variety of animals. These dishes would be accompanied by fantastic promises: 'Of great effectiveness is the sexual organ of a bull (especially when in rut). If one dries it, pulverises it and dissolves the powder in an egg, it has a wonderful effect.'

From Marinello, Italian doctor from the Renaissance period.

Cognac Lamb Chops

6 lamb chops (2–3 centimetres/1 inch thick)
6 anchovy fillets
6 rashers streaky bacon
25 g (1 oz or $^{1}/_{4}$ stick) butter for frying
4 medium-sized onions, finely chopped
2 cloves garlic, crushed
$^{1}/_{2}$ bunch parsley, chopped
1 bay leaf
fresh basil to taste
3–4 cloves
12 coriander seeds
2 tbs good cognac
2 tbs meat stock
salt and freshly ground pepper

Secure an anchovy fillet and rasher of bacon to each chop using a toothpick. Melt the butter in a pan; sweat the onions until they are translucent and fry the chops. Add the garlic, parsley, bay leaf, some basil, the cloves and coriander seeds. Add the cognac and stock. Season with salt and pepper and cook for 20 minutes.

Arrange the cutlets on the plates and pour over the sauce. Serve with rice.

Lemony Veal with Spring Vegetables

8 baby artichokes
juice of half a lemon
1 bunch spring onions (scallions)
4 thin veal cutlets
salt and pepper
olive oil
butter

Wash the artichokes, remove the hearts and rub them immediately with lemon juice to prevent them from browning. Simmer them in boiling salted water for 15 minutes. Steam the spring onions in salted water for 4–5 minutes and drain well.

Using a tenderiser or a rolling pin, lightly beat the veal into thin schnitzels and season with salt and pepper. Put the oil and butter in a frying pan and heat until the butter is foamy. Fry the veal for one minute on each side. Add some more butter and lemon juice, raise the heat and turn the schnitzel again. Arrange the schnitzels on a pre-warmed plate and serve with the artichokes and scallions.

Pork Roll–over

4 thin pork cutlets
salt and pepper
1 clove garlic, crushed
100 g (4 oz) fresh spinach
150 g (6 oz) button mushrooms
1 medium onion
50 g (2 oz or ½ stick) butter
grated nutmeg
150 g (6 oz) raw sausage meat
125 ml (½ cup) white wine
125 ml (½ cup) single (light) cream
1 tbs finely chopped parsley

Season the meat with salt, pepper and garlic. Blanch the spinach in boiling water for 1 minute, rinse in cold water and drain well. Clean the mushrooms and thinly slice them. Finely dice the onion and fry in some butter until the onion turns translucent. Add the spinach and sweat for 3 minutes. Season with salt, pepper and nutmeg. Spread the spinach mixture over each pork cutlet, and spread the sausage meat on top of the spinach. Roll each piece of meat up, and secure with a toothpick.

Heat the rest of the butter and fry the pork rolls, turning often. Add the mushrooms, cook for a couple of minutes and then pour some wine over the meat. Finally, add the cream and cook over a low heat for 20 minutes.

Take the rolls out of the pan, remove the toothpicks, and keep warm. Cook the sauce, adding pepper and parsley and stirring until it is thick and creamy. Serve the rolls with the sauce and rice or noodles.

Plummy Pork Fillets

2 lean pork cutlets or 4 pork fillets
freshly ground white pepper
sprig of thyme
2 plums (fresh or tinned)
250 ml (1 cup) marsala or white wine
50 g (2 oz or $1/2$ a stick) butter
salt
1 shallot, chopped
2 tsp redcurrants
2 tbs meat stock
1 tbs green peppercorns (ground)
cayenne pepper to taste

Season the meat with the pepper and the thyme. Halve the plums, remove the stone and slice them before marinating them in the marsala. Fry the meat in half the butter until it is golden brown and season it with salt. Remove excess fat from the frying pan before adding the shallots. Fry them briefly and add half the marsala marinade. Steam for 20 minutes. Take the meat out of the pan and keep warm.

Sieve the cooking juices and pour in the rest of the marsala. Turn the heat up high and reduce the liquid to half its original volume. Add the redcurrants, stock and peppercorns, cook for a couple of minutes and season with a couple of pinches of cayenne pepper. Finally, whisk the rest of the butter into the sauce. Warm the plum slices in the marsala sauce and garnish the meat with them.

To serve, ladle the sauce over the meat and serve with rice.

Bordeaux Steak

2 shallots or 1 onion
50 g (2 oz or ¹/₂ a stick) butter
125 ml (¹/₂ cup) meat stock
2 large marrow bones
250 ml (1 cup) red, preferably Bordeaux wine
2 entrecôte steaks
1 tbs oil
salt and freshly ground pepper
parsley to garnish

Finely chop one of the shallots and fry in 2 tablespoons of butter, stirring it regularly so that it does not brown. In a separate pan, bring the stock to a boil and add the marrow bones. Remove the pan from the heat, and leave the bones to stand for a while. Keep the stock warm, but ensure that the marrow remains pink and does not overcook. Meanwhile, chop the other shallot. Pour the red wine into a pan, add the shallot and cook over a high heat, reducing the volume of the liquid by half. Lightly brush the steaks in oil and either grill or fry them as long as you wish, depending on whether you like your meat rare or well done. Add the rest of the wine to the reduced liquid, and reduce it once more to half the original volume.

Season the cooked meat with salt and pepper and place the steaks on a pre-warmed plate. Remove the marrow from the bones, finely chop it and place half on each steak along with the chopped shallots. Whip the remaining butter into the sauce until the sauce is slightly creamy in texture, season with salt and pepper and pour over the steaks. Garnish with parsley, and serve the steaks with steamed vegetables or rice.

Fillet Steak Roquefort in Red Wine and Morel Sauce

3 dried morels or other wild mushrooms
1 ripe pear
125 ml ($^1/_2$ cup) red wine
2 thick cut fillet steaks (each weighing 225 g or $^1/_2$ lb)
50 g (2 oz) Roquefort cheese (or other strong blue cheese)
75 g (3 oz or $^3/_4$ stick) butter
salt and black pepper
mint leaves to garnish

Soak the morels in boiling water until they rehydrate and set aside. Peel the pear, halve it lengthways and remove the core. Poach it for a few minutes in the wine until it is warm. Put the pear aside and reserve the red wine for the sauce.

Cut a slit in the side of each steak to form a pocket in the middle of the meat. Dice the Roquefort and fill the pockets of the steaks with cheese. Secure the stuffing using toothpicks. Season both sides of the steaks with pepper and fry in one third of the butter for 2–3 minutes on each side. Remove the steaks from the pan, season them with salt and lay them on a warm plate. Cover with tin foil and keep warm.

Finely chop the morels and fry briefly in the steak juices. Add the red wine used for poaching the pear and reduce to 4–5 tablespoons volume. Whisk in the remaining butter until the sauce thickens and check the seasoning.

Next, cut the pear halves into a fan: slice the pear into thin slices, from the base of the fruit nearly to the top, but do not cut all the way. Spread the pear 'fan' on the plate and garnish with mint leaves. Serve the steak topped with the morel sauce with potato gratin.

Sexy Italian Saltimbocca

4 thin veal cutlets
freshly ground white pepper
4 slices Parma ham
4 sage leaves
2 tbs butter
1 knife-tip beef extract (such as Bovril)
salt to taste

Season the veal with the pepper. Top each cutlet with a slice of ham and a sage leaf, and secure with a toothpick. Fry both sides in butter, and then put aside and keep warm. Add 3–4 tablespoons of water to the cooking juices, add the beef extract and cook for a minute or two. Season (if necessary) with salt.

Put the saltimbocca on the plates and pour the sauce over them. Serve with mashed potato, risotto or steamed vegetables.

Moist Veal in Herb Sauce

450 g (1 lb) diced veal fillet
2 tbs butter
salt and freshly ground black pepper
4 tbs oil
1 tbs wine vinegar
2 hard-boiled eggs, finely chopped
4 tbs fresh mixed herbs (parsley, sage, mint, chives)

Fry the meat in the butter on a high heat, turning often so that all sides are sealed to keep the moisture in. Season with salt and pepper and fry on a low heat for a further 45 minutes, basting frequently with the cooking juices. Remove from the pan and leave it to 'relax' for a few minutes.

Combine the oil, vinegar, eggs, herbs, salt and pepper to form a sauce. Spoon the sauce over the veal, and serve warm with bread or rice.

Pork in a Pot

450 g (1 lb) lean pork fillet
4 or 5 rashers streaky bacon
2 tbs butter
salt and freshly ground white pepper
1 clove
1 onion, peeled
1 carrot
1 bay leaf
150 ml (scant ²/₃ cup) white wine
2 tbs double (heavy) cream
¹/₂ tsp cornflour

Preheat the oven to 200°C (400°F). Wrap the pork in the rashers of bacon to form a skin around the meat, and secure each rasher with a toothpick. Fry the fillet on the stove in an ovenproof dish very briefly in hot butter to seal it, and season with salt and pepper. Stick the clove into the whole onion, and add it to the pan, along with the carrot, which should be cut lengthways in half, and the bay leaf. Pour the wine over the meat and transfer to the oven. Bake for 20 minutes, basting the meat frequently so that it does not dry out. The meat should still be pink on the inside after 20 minutes.

Transfer the fillet to a heated plate. Add a few tablespoons of water to the cooking juices, place the roasting tin on the stove and bring the juices to a boil. Stir in the cornflour, stirring well to avoid lumps. Thicken the sauce with the cream and cook for a couple of minutes. Pour the sauce over the meat, and carve at the table. Serve with steamed baby vegetables and sautéed potatoes.

Spare Ribs Aflame

1 kg (2 lbs) spare ribs
4 tbs soy sauce
4 tbs oil
2 tbs tomato ketchup (catsup)
salt and freshly ground white pepper
3 tbs apricot conserve
1 piece of ginger (walnut-sized)
1 clove garlic

Wash the spare ribs, dry and carefully separate the rack with a sharp knife. Combine the soy sauce, oil, ketchup, salt, pepper and conserve. Peel the ginger and chop very finely, crush the garlic and mix both into the marinade. Thoroughly brush the spare ribs with the marinade and leave for at least 2 hours in the fridge. Grill or barbecue the spare ribs for 20–30 minutes, turning and basting them frequently.

Chilli Con Carne

100 g (4 oz) kidney beans or butter beans
150 g (6 oz) pork
1 onion
2 cloves garlic
1 tbs olive oil
1 small tin peeled plum tomatoes
1 carrot
1 stick celery
1 green pepper (capsicum)
150 g (6 oz) beef mince
125 ml ($^1/_2$ cup) red wine
200 ml (generous $^2/_3$ cup) meat stock
$^1/_2$ tsp chopped thyme
$^1/_2$ tsp chilli powder or 1–2 red chilli peppers to taste
2 tbs tomato purée concentrate
salt and freshly ground black pepper

Soak the beans overnight in water to soften them. Finely dice the pork and onion and finely chop the garlic. Heat some oil in a saucepan and carefully fry the onion and garlic until they are golden brown, taking care not to burn the garlic. Add the pork and fry for a couple of minutes and then add the tomatoes and their juices from the tin. Cover the pan and cook over a low heat for 15 minutes.

Peel the carrot and celery and finely dice. Remove the seeds from the green pepper and finely chop. Add the vegetables, mince, beans, wine and stock to the pan and season with thyme, chilli and tomato purée. Cover and cook on a low heat for 1 hour, or until the beans are soft, stirring frequently. If there is too much liquid in the chilli, remove the lid for the last 15 minutes.

Before serving, season with salt and black pepper and serve with bread or rice.

Pleased-to-meat-you Curry

450 g (1 lb) lamb shoulder (deboned)
1 onion
2 cloves garlic
50 g (2 oz or ½ stick) butter
1 tsp chilli powder or 1 red chilli pepper
2 tsp freshly ground black pepper
1 tsp ground caraway
2 tsp ground coriander (cilantro) seeds
2 tsp garam masala
1 tsp turmeric powder
2 small ripe tomatoes
juice of 1 lemon
salt
300 ml (1¼ cups) meat stock

Remove excess fat and fibres from the meat and dice into 2.5 centimetre (1 inch) cubes. Finely chop the onion and garlic and fry in butter until they are golden brown in colour. Add the chilli, pepper, caraway, coriander, garam masala and turmeric and fry, taking care not to burn the spices. Quarter the tomatoes and add them to the pan. When the tomatoes are cooked, add the meat with some lemon juice and salt and cook for around 15 minutes, stirring often so that the meat does not stick to the pan. Add a little water if necessary to prevent the spices from burning. Heat the stock and add it to the meat. Cook over a low heat for 1 hour, stirring often. Serve with rice.

LOVE BIRDS

In his 414BC comedy *The Birds*, the Greek poet Aristophanes mentioned an episode from ancient mythology in which the God of Love, Amor, hatched out of a silver egg. As soon as he emerged, he set the act of love in motion.

In all cultures, eggs symbolise fertility and vitality. The average chicken lays an extraordinary number of eggs in its lifetime, and the cockerel rules his roost with such potency. This is why the ancient Greeks put poultry at the top of any menu designed to celebrate Aphrodite, the Goddess of Love.

Aristotle noted that a sparrow 'in one hour coupled 83 times', and as a result, all sorts of mixtures of sparrow's brain and other aphrodisiac additions were widely used. Many women wished to eat the testicles and combs of young cockerels, in the belief that it would increase their sexual enjoyment, and this belief led to worrying massacres of the poultry population quite aside from the need for meat. The delicacies would be prepared in highly seasoned pasties, as Pierre de Bourdeille, Sier de Brantome (French writer, 1540–1614) reported:

'Of these finely mixed pasties, small cockerels, artichoke hearts, truffles or other inflaming delicacies many ladies make frequent use. When they eat these and fish around in the food, they dip their fork into it and take out either an artichoke, a truffle, a pistachio-nut or a comb of a cockerel and put it into their mouth, to which they say with a sad expression, "Miss!" Should they, however, catch an agreeable organ of a cockerel and get their teeth into it, they jubilantly cry, "Hit!"'

111

Delectable Duck Breast with Blood Orange Butter

4 blood oranges (whole)
1 tsp sugar
300 ml (1¹/₄ cups) duck gravy
2 tbs Campari Bitter
100 g (4 oz or 1 stick) butter, cubed
1 tbs green peppercorns
2 small duck breasts
salt and freshly ground white pepper

Grate the peel from three of the oranges, squeeze them and reserve the juice. Take 300 ml (1¹/₄ cups) orange juice, the zest, sugar and duck gravy and reduce over a high heat until it is a thick syrup. Add the Campari, cook for another minute, and strain the syrup through a sieve. Turn the heat down, and with a whisk beat in the butter a little at a time. Add the peppercorns, remove from the stove and keep the sauce warm in a sauce-boat.

Using a zester, peel the zest of the remaining orange in strips, cut into 2–3 centimetre (1 inch) pieces and blanch in hot water for a minute to soften them. Segment the orange, removing the skin and membranes between the segments. Reserve any juice and warm it with the orange pieces in a pan.

Score the skin of the duck in a diamond pattern, without piercing the meat, and season with salt and pepper. Fry the breast on the skin side first, so that the excess fat melts, and then fry the other side briefly until it is cooked pink (the duck should not be overcooked). Allow the duck to relax for 5 minutes before serving and then cut diagonally into strips. Garnish with the orange butter, orange segments and zest.

Serve with mangetout beans (snow peas), fine angel hair pasta, or potato gratin.

'Coconutty About You' Chicken

1 kg (2 lbs) whole chicken
500 ml (2 generous cups) coconut milk
salt
4 cloves garlic
1 tbs roasted peanuts
1 tbs caraway seeds
1 tbs ground coriander (cilantro) seeds
4 black peppercorns
1 tsp grated lemon rind
1 tbs Vietnamese fish sauce (nuoc mam)
2 tsp chilli
2 tbs soy sauce
1 tbs shrimp paste
1 tsp sugar

Place the chicken in a large saucepan and add the coconut milk and a little salt. Cover and cook over a low heat for 1 hour and 10 minutes. Take the chicken out of the saucepan, remove the bones, and keep warm. Return the pan to the heat and reduce the cooking juices to half the original volume.

Blend the garlic, peanuts, caraway, coriander and peppercorns in a liquidiser. Stir the remaining ingredients into the blended mixture and cook until the sauce is thick and creamy. Add more salt if necessary. Serve the warm chicken on two plates with the sauce and saffron rice.

Bronzed Chicken Breast in Lime Sauce

2–3 limes
1 tbs sugar
250 ml (1 cup) chicken stock
150 ml (generous $^1\!/_2$ cup) single (light) cream
2 chicken breasts (including the skin and breast bone)
salt and freshly ground white pepper
2 tbs butter
lemon balm leaves to garnish

Pre-heat the oven to 250°C (480°F). Wash the limes and grate about 1 teaspoon of zest. Using a zester, peel off the rest of the rind and cut into small pieces. Squeeze the juice from the limes and cook with the grated rind, sugar and stock until the sauce is syrupy in consistency. Add the cream, and reduce to half the original volume. Blanch the strips of lime zest in hot water for a couple of minutes and set aside.

Season the chicken breasts with salt and pepper. Spread 1 tablespoon of butter in a baking tin and lay the chicken breasts on top. Bake in the oven for 12 minutes, turning them frequently until they are golden brown but still moist inside. Remove the bones and keep the chicken warm.

Finish the sauce in the baking tin – place the tin on the stove, add the sauce made earlier and bring to the boil, skimming off any scum that develops while boiling. Pass through a fine sieve and work in the rest of the butter. Add some salt if necessary. Cut the meat diagonally into strips. Arrange the chicken on the plate, add the lime zest to the sauce and pour over the chicken, and garnish with the lemon balm leaves. Serve with pasta.

Spanish Saffron Chicken

1 kg (2 lbs) chicken quarters
salt and freshly ground white pepper
2 tbs olive oil
100 g (¼ lb) cured ham (Serrano or Parma)
1 clove garlic
½ g (large pinch) saffron strands
1 sprig parsley
1 tbs flour
2 tsp white wine
400 ml (1¾ cups) chicken stock
grated nutmeg
200 g (1½ cups) fresh peas
2 hard-boiled eggs
2 slices bread
½ tbs butter

Separate the thighs and drumsticks, season the chicken with salt and pepper and fry in oil. Slice the ham into thin strips, add them to the pan and fry with the chicken for 1–2 minutes. Crush the garlic and add it to the pan, along with the saffron and parsley. Dust the chicken with flour and allow the flour time to absorb excess juices. Add the wine and stock and simmer on a medium heat until the chicken is cooked.

Take the chicken pieces out of the sauce and keep warm. Reduce the sauce to half its volume and season with nutmeg.

Meanwhile, blanch the peas in hot water, and rinse with cold water so they keep their colour. Halve the hard-boiled eggs, force the egg yolks through a sieve and mix them into the sauce. Sieve the sauce and add the peas. Allow them to warm through in the sauce, and finally pour over the chicken pieces.

Cut the slices of bread into triangles, butter and toast them under the grill. Chop up the egg whites and sprinkle them over the saffron chicken. Garnish with the bread. Serve immediately, with rice as a side dish.

Tender Chicken in Turmeric Sauce

2 large chicken thighs
salt and freshly ground white pepper
1 tbs flour
butter for frying
medium-sized banana
1 tsp chopped pistachios

For the sauce:
1 tbs butter
1 tbs onion, finely chopped
$^1/_2$ small cooking apple
$^1/_2$ tsp paprika
1 tsp turmeric powder
125 ml ($^1/_2$ cup) white port
200 ml (generous $^3/_4$ cup) chicken stock
1 tsp flour-butter (soft butter with flour kneaded into it)
200 ml (generous $^3/_4$ cup) heavy (double) cream
1 tsp honey
1 tbs mango chutney

Season the chicken thighs with salt and pepper and coat them in flour. Fry the pieces in butter until they are golden brown. Remove the chicken from the pan and drain all the excess fat.

For the sauce, add fresh butter to the pan and fry the onions until they are golden brown. Peel the apple, remove the core, finely chop half of it and add to the onions. Fry briefly before lowering the heat. Add the paprika, turmeric, port and stock while stirring thoroughly. Bring to the boil and return the chicken to the pan, reduce the heat and simmer uncovered for 15 minutes.

Take the chicken out of the pan and keep warm, allowing the meat to relax for 10 minutes. Meanwhile bring the sauce to the boil, carefully remove the fat and reduce over a high heat. Stir the flour–butter into the sauce and allow it to thicken. Add the cream and reduce once more until the sauce is thick and creamy. Add the honey, salt and pepper and sieve the sauce. Add the chicken to the sauce along with the chutney and bring to the boil again.

Peel the banana, cut into thin slices lengthways and fry in butter until golden brown. Arrange the chicken and sauce on a pre-warmed plate, place the bananas on the side of the chicken and garnish with the chopped pistachios. Serve with buttery rice.

Chicken Crêpes Madeira

For the crêpes:
50 g (2 oz) white flour
125 ml (half cup) milk
2 eggs
pinch of salt
pinch of sugar
$^1/_2$ tbs butter, melted
butter for frying

For the filling:
1 tbs butter
150 g (6 oz) stewing chicken
80 g (3 oz) chicken liver, finely chopped
salt and freshly ground black pepper
300 ml ($1^1/_4$ cups) Madeira wine
100 ml (scant $^1/_2$ cup) poultry stock
1 tbs single (light) cream
1 tsp marjoram and thyme, finely chopped
1 tbs chopped parsley

For the crêpe batter, place the flour in a glass dish and whisk in the milk until there are no lumps. Work in the eggs, a pinch of salt, sugar and butter, whisking the batter well. Leave to stand for 1–2 hours in the refrigerator. To make four crêpes, use a small, well-buttered pan, pour a quarter of the mixture into the pan and spread evenly. When the mixture has set, flip the crêpe and cook for less than a minute. Repeat three times. Lay the crêpes on top of each other, separating each one with kitchen paper and keep them warm.

For the filling, heat the butter in a pan. Season the chicken and liver with salt and pepper and fry on a high heat for a few minutes, then remove the meat and keep in a warm place. Pour any remaining fat from the pan and add the Madeira and stock. Reduce the sauce until it is quite thick in consistency. Add the cream, and cook until the sauce thickens once more. Season with the herbs, and add the chicken and liver to warm up again.

Remove the crêpes from the oven, divide the filling between them, and roll up. Serve immediately.

GAME FOR GAME

For difficult cases of impotency, the student of magic, Caterina da Forli, recommended in her secret book of recipes: 'Eat the testicles of a deer or the tip of the brush of a fox and its testicles, as this inflames the desire of a woman. Also, if the rod of a man is rubbed with the gall of a boar or wild pig this provokes immediate lust in women.'

Rack of Hare Caressed with Calvados

1 rack of hare (450 g or 1 lb)
125 ml ($^1/_2$ cup) white wine
$^1/_2$ onion, coarsely chopped
1 bay leaf
$^1/_2$ tsp dried oregano
salt and freshly ground black pepper
1 tbs butter
pinch of grated nutmeg
3 tbs Calvados
4 tbs cider
125 ml ($^1/_2$ cup) game stock
2 tbs double (heavy) cream
cayenne pepper to taste

Carefully remove the fillets from inside of the rack of hare. Boil the white wine, onion, bay leaf, oregano, salt and pepper in a saucepan. Lay the rack and fillets in a glass bowl, add the wine mixture and marinate in the fridge overnight.

Remove the rack and fillets from the marinade and fry in butter until they are golden in colour. Remove the fillets from the pan. Season the rack with a little more salt, pepper and nutmeg, cover the pan and cook for a further 15 minutes over a low heat. Pour the Calvados over the rack and flambé to remove any excess alcohol. Remove the rack and keep warm while making the sauce. Add the cider and stock, cream and a pinch of cayenne pepper and cook until the sauce has thickened slightly.

Serve the meat and the sauce separately with potatoes or rice.

Wild Boar with Baby Onions

450 g (1 lb) wild boar fillets
salt and freshly ground white pepper
5 tbs oil
2 medium onions
3 tbs tomato purée
300 ml (1¹/₄ cups) red wine
100 ml (scant ¹/₂ cup) game stock
8 juniper berries, crushed
15 baby onions
4 slices streaky bacon

Dice the meat into cubes approximately 2.5 centimetres (1 inch) long and season with salt and pepper. Heat the oil and fry the meat, turning it regularly. Finely dice the onions and fry them until they are translucent. Stir in the tomato purée, pour in the wine and stock and add the juniper berries. Cook on a low heat for 45 minutes. In the last 10 minutes of cooking time, add the baby onions. Cut the bacon into thin strips, fry them in a pan separately until they are crispy and then sprinkle them over the stew.

Serve with dumplings or rice and red cabbage.

Venison and Celery Sensation

4 venison fillets
freshly ground black pepper
$^1/_4$ tsp marjoram
5 medium potatoes
half a head of celery
2 tbs butter
1 cooking apple
125 ml ($^1/_2$ cup) white wine
2 tbs lemon juice
salt
1 tbs cognac
100 ml (scant $^1/_2$ cup) game stock
150 ml ($^2/_3$ cup) double (heavy) cream
2 tbs fresh cranberries

Season both sides of the fillets with pepper and marjoram, and leave to sit for 15 minutes. Peel and slice the potatoes and boil in salted water until done. Peel the celery and cook in salted water for 10 minutes until it is soft. Reserve the cooking liquid. Fry the celery in half the butter for a couple of minutes until all excess moisture has evaporated. Purée the potatoes and the celery in a blender.

Peel and halve the apple, and boil in 100 millilitres (half a cup) of water and half the white wine and lemon juice, until parboiled.

Fry the venison in the rest of the butter until golden in colour and lightly salt the meat. Place on a warmed plate and keep warm. Add the cognac, the rest of the white wine and stock to the meat juices and bring to the boil. Mix in two-thirds of the cream and add half the cranberries.

Combine the rest of the cream with 1 tablespoon of the celery water in a small pan and bring to the boil. Add the celery and potato purée and stir well. Warm the purée and add a knob of butter and more salt if necessary.

Stuff the apple halves with the rest of the berries. Pour the sauce over the venison, and serve with the mashed celery and potatoes and the apple halves.

Venison Adorned with Figs and Grapes

450 g (1 lb) rack of venison
salt and freshly ground black pepper
2 tsp sweet paprika
125 g (5 oz or 1¼ sticks) butter
3 tbs game juices
3 tbs red wine
4 fresh figs
100 g (4 oz) green grapes
100 g (4 oz) red grapes

Season the meat with salt, pepper and paprika. Melt one-fifth of the butter in a roasting tin, put the venison in the tin and roast for 15–20 minutes at 200°C (400°F).

Meanwhile, heat the game juices in a pan and add the wine. Stirring frequently, cook until the sauce has reduced to half its original volume. Remove the pan from the heat and allow to cool for a few minutes. Dice nearly all the remaining the butter and whisk it a little at a time into the sauce. Season with salt and pepper.

Halve the figs and heat them, along with the grapes, with the last bit of butter. Take the venison out of the roasting tin when it is ready. Carefully remove the meat from both sides of the ribs and cut into slices about 1 centimetre (½ inch) thick.

Add a little water to the roasting tin, scraping the tin with a wooden spoon. Sieve the wine and stock liquid straight into the tin and cook for a couple more minutes.

Arrange the meat on two warmed plates and garnish with the warm figs and grapes. Serve the sauce separately with pasta.

Venison Steak Bliss

2 venison steaks
4 slices streaky smoked bacon
2 tbs oil
1 tbs mixed wild herbs
salt and freshly ground black pepper

Remove any fibres and excess fat from the steaks and cut into round fillets (tournedos) about 4 centimetres (1½ inches) thick. Wrap the bacon around the sides of the steaks and secure with toothpicks. Sprinkle a little oil on both sides of the steaks and coat them in the herbs, salt and pepper. Cover and leave to marinate in the fridge for 1 hour.

Heat some oil in a pan and seal the steaks over a high heat for 2 minutes on each side. Reduce the heat and fry for another 5 minutes so that they are cooked pink. Serve immediately.

The steaks can be served with pasta, noodles or wild mushrooms.

Creamy Venison Cutlet

4 small venison cutlets
1 tbs flour
1 tbs butter
salt and freshly ground pepper
100 g (4 oz) mushrooms
500 ml (2 cups) good red wine
100 ml (scant ½ cup) double (heavy) cream

Coat the meat in a little flour. Fry briefly in very hot butter and season with salt and pepper. Remove the meat from the pan and keep it warm. Fry the mushrooms in the cooking juices and add the wine. Simmer for 15 minutes, season if necessary and add the cream. Warm the sauce but do not let it boil, pour over the meat and serve. Serve with mashed potatoes and braised red cabbage.

VIRGINAL VEGETARIANS

'There are some fruits that refresh, but there are also a great many which make one hot, and unfortunately, it is to these that women most often reach. They reach to the various greens that are in flower and taste good in soups and salads, such as: asparagus, artichokes, morels, truffles and other mushrooms. Furthermore, their cooks on their bidding knew how to prepare the new spices deliciously, and serve very well; these spices are also busily prescribed by doctors. After these wonderful dishes take care, you poor lovers and husbands! Can you not foresee, that your honour is done for, and you will be exchanged and deceived?'

Pierre de Bordeille, Sieur de Brantome,
French writer (1540–1614).

Seduce me with... Spinach and Ricotta Gnocchi

5 tbs butter
400 g (14 oz) leaf spinach
150 g (5 oz) ricotta cheese
2 eggs
80 g (3 oz) flour
100 g (4 oz) grated parmesan or pecorino cheese
pinch grated nutmeg
salt and freshly ground black pepper

Heat 2 tablespoons of the butter in a frying pan and sweat the spinach over a low heat for 2 minutes, until the spinach juices have evaporated. Press the spinach over a sieve to remove excess juices, and then add the ricotta. Stir in the eggs, flour and a quarter of the grated cheese. Season with nutmeg, salt and pepper and leave the mixture to cool for about half an hour. Bring plenty of salted water to the boil.

Coat your hands in flour and fashion the mixture into little balls. Carefully place the balls into the lightly simmering water to cook for 5–8 minutes. (It is a good idea to do a test-run with one gnocchi ball – if the mixture does not hold together properly, add a little more flour.)

Once cooked, remove the gnocchi with a slotted spoon and drain well. Grease an oven dish with 2 tablespoons of melted butter, put the gnocchi in the dish and sprinkle over the rest of the cheese. Finally, finely cube the rest of the butter and place on top of the cheese. Bake in a 200°C (400°F) oven until the cheese has melted. Serve with salad.

'Women who hate potatoes are frigid and uptight. Potato lovers give their lovers hours of lustful pleasure and are never ill tempered.'

Kiichi Kurijama

Scrumptious Gnocchi with Juicy Sage Butter

450 g (1 lb) boiled potatoes
1 egg
salt
75–150 g (3–6 oz) flour
100 g (4 oz) grated parmesan or pecorino cheese

For the sauce:
75 g (3 oz) butter
12 sage leaves
salt and pepper

Boil the potatoes in their skins until they are floury in texture. While they are still warm, peel their skins and mash. When the mash has cooled a little, add the egg, a pinch of salt and enough flour so that when kneaded, the mixture does not stick to your hands – add as much flour as the potatoes need to absorb. Roll the dough into a finger-thick sausage and cut into 2–3 centimetre (1 inch) pieces. Lay each piece over a fork, press lightly and roll slightly – the sauce will adhere more effectively to the indentations. Bring some salted water to the boil and put the gnocchi into the water. They will float when they are ready. Remove them with a slotted spoon, and drain well. Put on a serving plate and keep warm.

For the sauce, warm the butter, finely chop the sage leaves and add them, seasoning the butter with salt and pepper. Cook on a low heat for a couple of minutes. Pour over the gnocchi and sprinkle with the cheese.

Variations: Instead of the sage butter, you can serve the gnocchi with pesto, or with fresh basil butter (substitute the sage for basil and garlic), or serve with a simple tomato and herb sauce.

Mushrooms are rich in vitamins and minerals, which makes them essential to any lovers' menu. But it is also because, like love, they grow mysteriously in the darkness of night, appearing as if from nowhere by morning.

Papardelle with Black Truffles

1–2 black truffles (fresh or tinned)
75 g (3 oz or ³/₂ stick) butter
salt and freshly ground black pepper
2 tbs dry white wine
100 g (scant ¹/₂ cup) single (light) cream
300 g (12 oz) fresh papardelle (wide, ribbon noodles)

Slice the truffles into wafer-thin strips. Heat the butter until it is foaming, reduce the heat and sweat the truffles over a low heat for a few minutes. Season with freshly ground black pepper and a little salt.

Remove the truffles from the pan and set aside. Add the wine and cream to the pan and cook on a low heat until the sauce is thick and creamy.

In the meantime, cook the noodles until they are 'al dente' (not overdone). Mix the truffles back into the sauce and season with salt and pepper. Pour liberally over the noodles and serve immediately.

Alluring Aubergine Parmigiana

2 large, firm aubergines (eggplant)
salt
1 can plum tomatoes
1/2 onion
bunch of basil leaves
olive oil for frying
2 cakes buffalo mozzarella cheese
2 eggs
freshly ground black pepper
6 tbs grated parmesan or pecorino cheese

Cut the aubergines into round slices approximately 1 centimetre (1/2 inch) thick. Rub the slices with plenty of salt and stack them on top of each other on a plate. Cover and place a weight on the top of the stack. Leave for 1–2 hours; this is so that the bitter juices can be extracted from the aubergines.

In the meantime, make the tomato sauce. Heat the tomatoes in a saucepan. Finely chop the onion and add it to the tomatoes, along with some basil leaves. Stir occasionally, and cook until the sauce has reduced and thickened slightly. Add a little salt when the sauce is cooked, and remove from the heat.

Rinse the aubergine slices of the salt and pat them dry with kitchen paper. Heat the olive oil and fry the slices a few at a time on both sides, until they are golden brown. When they are cooked, put them on a kitchen paper to absorb excess oil.

Chop the mozzarella and the rest of the basil leaves. Mix the eggs, salt, pepper and eight tablespoons of the tomato sauce into the mozzarella and basil.

Lay one-third of the aubergines in a fireproof dish and cover with about three tablespoons of the tomato sauce. Next, spoon a thin layer of the mozzarella mixture over the sauce. Put another layer of aubergines on top of the sauce, and keep on layering the ingredients in the same order until there are three layers. If the aubergines on the top of the dish are not fully covered, use the rest of the tomato sauce to make sure that the aubergines are not exposed. Finally, top the sauce with grated parmesan cheese and bake in an oven pre-heated to 180°C (350°F) for 45 minutes.

Serve with Spring-in-your-step Salad (page 49).

'Whoever eats a lot of asparagus, will have many lovers.'
Traditional German folk saying.

Asparagus with Hollandaise Sauce

750 g (1¹/₂ lb) white asparagus
pinch of sugar
2 tbs butter
450 g (1 lb) baby new potatoes
2 tbs breadcrumbs

For the hollandaise sauce:
125 g (6 oz or 1¹/₂ sticks) cold butter
2 egg yolks
lemon juice
2 tbs white wine or water
pinch of cayenne pepper
salt and freshly ground black pepper

Wash and peel the asparagus and remove the ends of the stalks. Leave it to stand in boiling salted water with a pinch of sugar and a little butter for no longer than 25 minutes. Remove the asparagus and wrap in kitchen cloth, so that it is kept warm and the excess moisture is absorbed.

Boil the potatoes in their skins for 20 minutes, or until they are ready, and then peel the skin off. Fry the breadcrumbs in melted butter until they are light brown in colour. Reserve the cooking fat to coat the potatoes before serving.

For the sauce, dice the butter into small cubes. Stir the egg yolk with a little lemon juice and the wine in a metal basin. Place the basin in a moderately warm bain-marie and beat the sauce until it is foamy. The water should not be too hot or the sauce will curdle. Gradually add the butter a little at a time and whisk thoroughly, making sure that the last lot of butter has melted before adding more. When all the butter has melted, remove the sauce from the bain-marie and season with cayenne pepper, black pepper, salt and some lemon juice. Serve the asparagus and the sauce separately.

If one believes the Greek doctor, Dioskurides, carrots can lead to adulterous liaisons. In East Asia, carrots are a substitute for ginseng, a well-known and expensive aphrodisiac. In an ancient cookery book it is written: 'The yellow root, the carrot, will bring lust to conjugal matters. Spiced with parsley, this lust will be heightened still more.'

Moroccan Carrots

1 bunch carrots
3 cloves garlic, halved
$^1/_2$ bunch parsley
1–2 sprigs mint
salt and freshly ground black pepper
1 tbs oil
1 tbs vinegar
1 tsp ground caraway or to taste

Peel the carrots and cut into slices about 1 centimetre ($^1/_2$ inch) thick. Boil the carrots and garlic in salted water, so they are still slightly crunchy. Meanwhile, chop the parsley and mint. Leave the carrots to cool and season with salt, pepper, oil and vinegar. Add the herbs and the caraway, mix and serve.

Fennel and Wild Rice Bouquet

2 heads fennel
100 g (3½ oz) wild rice
salt
100 g (3½ oz) long grain rice
1 shallot
50 g (2 oz or ½ stick) butter
pepper
2 tbs sherry
1–2 tbs roasted pine kernels
6 nasturtium flowers as a decorative garnish

Remove the fennel leaves and set aside. Cook the fennel in salted water for 20 minutes. In a separate saucepan add the wild rice to boiling water with a pinch of salt. After 10 minutes add the long grain rice and cook for a further 20 minutes.

Halve the fennel and hollow out the insides. Dice the shallot and fry in butter, along with the fennel. Add the drained rice and season with salt, pepper, sherry and the fennel leaves. Stuff the halves of the fennel with this mixture, garnish with pine kernels and the nasturtiums and serve immediately.

Intoxicating Braised Celery

4 sticks celery
250 ml (1 cup) white wine
3 tbs mixed chopped herbs (parsley, chervil, chives)
salt and freshly ground black pepper
4 tbs breadcrumbs
4 tbs soft butter

Slice the celery into bite-sized pieces. Blanch for 3 minutes in hot salted water. Pour the wine and herbs into an oven-proof dish. Add the celery and season with salt and pepper. Mix the breadcrumbs and the butter together and spread over the vegetables.

Bake for 20–25 minutes in an oven that has been pre-heated to 200°C (400°F).

Variation: Instead of the breadcrumbs and the butter, substitute Roquefort cheese on the celery for a fuller flavour.

Country Radish Curry

1 large white radish (mooli)
2 small onions
1 clove garlic
1 beef tomato
1 tbs butter
1 tbs curry powder
freshly ground black pepper
$^1/_2$ tsp ground caraway
1 tsp grated ginger
salt
soy sauce to taste
2 tbs chopped cashew nuts
100 ml (scant $^1/_2$ cup) full fat yogurt
1 tsp lemon juice
$^1/_4$ bunch flat leaf parsley

Slice the radish into pieces about 3 centimetres (1$^1/_4$ inches) long and $^1/_2$ centimetre ($^1/_4$ inch) thick). Chop the onions and garlic very finely. Boil the tomato whole, peel off its skin and finely dice.

Melt the butter in a saucepan and carefully fry the curry powder, pepper and caraway, taking care not to burn the mixture. Add the onions, garlic and ginger, and cook for a further 5 minutes. Add the radish, salt and some soy sauce and cook for a further 15 minutes. Finally, add the tomato, nuts, yogurt and lemon juice and cook for 2 minutes. Garnish the curry with plenty of parsley leaves.

Randy Ratatouille

4 tomatoes
1 yellow pepper
1 red pepper
1 small aubergine (eggplant)
2 small courgettes (zucchini)
2 medium-sized onions
2 cloves garlic
3 tbs olive oil
salt and freshly ground black pepper
1–2 tbs chopped mixed fresh herbs (thyme, rosemary,
oregano, basil, parsley)

Remove the skins and seeds from the tomatoes and coarsely chop the flesh. Slice the rest of the vegetables into thin batons. Chop the onions and garlic and fry them in the olive oil. Add the peppers and aubergines and fry for 10 minutes, stirring frequently. Add the tomatoes and courgettes and cook for another 10 minutes without the lid, so that the ratatouille is not too liquid. Season with salt, pepper and chopped herbs, and finally cook for another 15 minutes before serving.

Potato and Courgette Gratin

1–2 small courgettes (zucchini)
450 g (1 lb) parboiled potatoes
1 clove garlic
1 tbs butter
1 onion
200 ml (³/₄ cup) double (heavy) cream
100 ml (scant ¹/₂ cup) veal, chicken or vegetable stock
salt and freshly ground black pepper
pinch of grated nutmeg
40 g (1¹/₂ oz) grated Emmental cheese

Slice the courgettes into round pieces about 5 millimetres (¹/₄ inch) thick. Peel the potatoes and cut into thin slices. Rub a cake tin with half a clove of garlic and grease with some butter. Layer the potatoes and courgettes in the tin, overlapping each other slightly. Peel the onion, dice and fry it in butter until translucent, taking care not to let it brown. Add the cream and stock and season with salt, pepper and nutmeg. Pour the onion and stock mixture over the vegetables and sprinkle the cheese on top. Bake in an oven pre-heated to 150°C (300°F) for 40 minutes, or until the top of the gratin is golden brown.

Glazed Turnip with Nuts

450 g (1 lb) turnips
2–3 tbs walnut oil
salt and freshly ground black pepper
grated nutmeg
3 tbs chopped walnuts
5–6 tbs vegetable stock
125 ml ($^1/_2$ cup) whipped cream

Remove the leaves and roots from the turnips and peel. Leave the smaller turnips whole and quarter the larger ones. Fry them in the oil for 5 minutes. Season with salt, pepper and nutmeg, and add the nuts and stock. Cook over a low heat for 30 minutes. Finally, stir in the whipped cream, warm and serve.

Kohlrabi in a Piquant Sauce

2 large kohlrabi
1 bunch spring onions (scallions)
1 tbs butter
100 ml (scant $^1/_2$ cup) soured cream
salt and freshly ground white pepper
1 tsp lemon juice
pinch of sugar
pinch of grated nutmeg

Remove the leaves and set aside. Remove and discard the roots, peel and quarter the kohlrabi. Slice each quarter very thinly. Chop the spring onions into very thin slices right up to the older green leaves at the top.

In a large pan, melt the butter and fry the kohlrabi for 5 minutes. Add the spring onions and cook for a short time before stirring in the cream. Season with salt, pepper, lemon juice, sugar and nutmeg. Cook for a few more minutes over a low heat.

Garnish with the kohlrabi leaves that were removed earlier and serve with rice or boiled potatoes.

CLIMAX!

' A most unusual type of table decoration originated that served the English and the French for a long time: it was a representation of the male and female sexual organs, made of dough and sugar. These were presented to guests at banquets, and were undoubtedly intended to stimulate jokes and conversation...'

Footnote: R. Warner in *Antiquitates culinariae* (1791).

Melt-in-your-mouth Strawberries and Wine Mousse

200 g (7 oz) strawberries
1 tbs sugar
1 tsp lemon juice

For the wine mousse:
125 g ($^1/_2$ cup) whipping or double (heavy) cream
2 egg yolks
3 tsp sugar
$^1/_2$ tsp grated lemon rind
pinch of grated nutmeg
1 tbs cognac
grated chocolate to garnish

Halve the strawberries and dust with the sugar and lemon juice. Divide between two large fluted glasses and keep cool until serving.

For the mousse, whisk the cream until it is stiff and put it in the fridge. Shortly before serving, create a bain-marie by placing a high-sided basin over a pan of hot water and place the egg yolks, sugar, lemon rind, nutmeg and cognac in it. Keep the pan on a low heat and whisk the ingredients into a foam. Leave to cool for 1–2 minutes, fold in the cream and serve with the strawberries. Sprinkle with grated chocolate just before serving.

Poached Pears for a Pair

500 ml (2 cups) muscat wine
$^1/_2$ nutmeg
$^1/_2$ stick cinnamon
1 large bay leaf
juice of $^1/_2$ lemon
1 tbs finely chopped ginger
1 tsp cloves
1 tsp cardamom seeds
1 tsp pimento seeds
1 vanilla pod
2 pears with stems
$^1/_2$ tsp cinnamon powder
$^1/_2$ tsp grated nutmeg (or to taste)
$^1/_2$ tsp powdered pimento
$^1/_2$ tsp ground ginger
$^1/_2$ tsp clove powder
$^1/_2$ tsp vanilla extract
1 tbs sugar
200 ml (generous $^3/_4$ cup) whipping cream
to garnish: mint leaves

Pour the wine into a saucepan and add the nutmeg, cinnamon, bay leaf, lemon juice, ginger, cloves, cardamom, pimento and the vanilla pod, which should be sliced open. Simmer for 30 minutes.

In the meantime, peel the pears. Strain the spiced wine through a sieve. Place the pears in the liquid and poach for 10–20 minutes, or until the pears are soft. Place one pear on the centre of a large plate and spoon a little – not too much – of the juice around the pear. Leave the pears to cool.

Add the powdered spices (cinnamon, nutmeg, pimento, ginger and cloves), vanilla extract and the sugar to the cream and whip until it is stiff. Serve with the pears and garnish with mint leaves.

Citrus Captured by Cream Jelly

125 ml ($^1/_2$ cup) whipping cream
1 tbs caster (superfine) sugar
1 piece candied ginger in syrup
2 sheets white gelatine
2 tbs orange juice
2 tbs brazil nuts
1 orange
1 blood orange
1 mandarin
to garnish: candied orange

Whip the cream until it is almost, but not quite stiff, and fold in 1 tablespoon sugar and 1 tablespoon ginger syrup. Soften the gelatine in cold water for about 10 minutes and drain well. Dissolve the gelatine in the orange juice over a very low heat, allow it to cool a little, and then fold thoroughly into the cream. Add sugar to taste.

Finely chop the nuts and ginger and fold into the cream. Fill two individual jelly (jello) moulds and chill for at least 6 hours. Peel the oranges and cut into slices. Peel the mandarin and separate into segments, removing the film that covers each segment. Empty the moulds onto each plate, sprinkle with candied orange and arrange the fruit attractively around the jellies.

Sweet-as-you Banana Flan

2 bananas
3 eggs
500 ml (2 cups) milk
1 tbs sugar
salt
$^1/_2$ tsp vanilla essence
$^1/_2$ tsp grated lemon rind
1 tsp butter

Peel the bananas and slice into pieces 2–3 centimetres (1 inch) long. Whisk the eggs, add the milk and mix in the sugar, a pinch of salt, vanilla essence and lemon rind. Grease a fireproof flan dish and pour in the egg mixture. Arrange the banana pieces vertically in the mixture. Cook in an oven pre-heated to 200°C (400°F). The flan should not be too firm when it is taken out, and it can be served warm or chilled.

Up-all-night Espresso Mousse

3 egg whites
60 g (2 oz) sugar
2 tsp dark rum
4 tbs freshly brewed espresso
1 sheet gelatine
125 ml (¹/₂ cup) whipping cream
coffee powder to dust

Whisk the egg whites and sugar into a soft foam, taking care not to over-whisk.

Stir 1 teaspoon of rum into the hot espresso and fold into the egg whites. Using a whisk, beat the espresso and egg whites until the mixture cools. Soak the gelatine in cold water and dry it well. Dissolve the gelatine in the remaining rum over a low heat. Thoroughly fold into the egg and espresso mixture. Put the mixture in the fridge and leave to cool for about 20 minutes so that the mixture can set.

Whip the cream until it stands in stiff peaks and carefully fold two-thirds of it into the set mixture. Fill two ramekins with the mousse and put them in the freezer for 15 minutes prior to serving. Just before the mousse is served, top with the rest of the cream and dust with a little coffee powder.

Plump Plums in White Wine

450 g (1 lb) fresh plums
1 tbs lemon juice
2 tbs caster sugar
300 ml (1¹/₄ cups) white wine

Blanch the plums in hot water, and peel the skins. Halve each plum, remove the pits, and slice. Sprinkle the lemon juice and sugar on the plums, pour the white wine over them and leave to marinate in the fridge for 2–3 hours before serving.

Exotic Rosehip Pudding with Fruit Salad

For the cream:
400 ml (1¹/₂ cups) milk
1 packet of vanilla instant pudding mix
1 egg (separated)
2 tbs sugar
salt
1 tsp ground ginger
3 tbs unsweetened rosehips (available health food shops)
rind of 1 orange
100 ml (scant ¹/₂ cup) whipping cream

For the fruit salad:
2 oranges
100 g (4 oz) kumquats
1 pomegranate
1 apple
2 tbs orange liqueur or orange juice

For the sauce:
rind and juice of 1 lime
2 tbs sugar
1 packet vanilla sugar

Cook the milk, pudding mix, egg yolk, sugar and a pinch of salt. Once the mixture is warmed and beginning to thicken, add the ginger, rosehips and orange rind. Beat the egg white into stiff peaks and fold into the pudding. Leave the mixture to cool. Whip the cream until it is stiff, and then carefully fold into the mixture.

For the fruit salad, separate the oranges into segments, removing the membrane around each section and reserving any juice that results. Wash and halve the kumquats. Halve the pomegranate and remove the seeds. Peel and core the apple and cut into pieces. Steam the fruit for 3 minutes in the reserved orange juice and liqueur and then leave to cool.

To make the sauce, take the grated lime rind and juice, and stir in the sugar and vanilla sugar. Pour over the prepared fruit and serve with the rosehip pudding.

Sensuous Zabaglione with Vanilla Ice Cream

3 tbs caster (superfine) sugar
3 egg whites
150 ml (generous ¹/₂ cup) marsala wine
2 large scoops vanilla ice cream

Create a bain-marie – place a high-sided basin over a pan of simmering water. Put the sugar and egg whites in the basin and whisk into a soft foam. Add the wine and stir continuously until the mixture is foamy and has thickened.

Serve straight away in a sundae glass, with a scoop of ice cream with each serving.

Tantalising Tiramisu

150 ml (generous ¹/₂ cup) espresso or strong coffee
2 tbs dark rum (or more, according to taste)
100 g (4 oz) sponge cake fingers
1 tbs cocoa powder

For the cream:
4 eggs (separated)
¹/₂ tsp vanilla essence
100 g (3¹/₂ oz) caster (superfine) sugar
300 g (¹/₂ cup) mascarpone cheese

Brew the coffee and leave it to cool. Stir in the rum and leave to cool.

Beat the egg yolks, vanilla essence and sugar into a thick, runny cream, add the mascarpone and mix well. Beat the egg whites until they form stiff peaks and carefully fold into the egg yolk mixture.

Arrange half of the sponge fingers in the bottom of a glass serving bowl and moisten them with the rum. Spread half the mixture over the fingers, place another layer of fingers over the cream, and repeat once more. Leave to chill in the fridge for 4–6 hours. Shortly before serving, dust the top of the tiramisu with cocoa powder.

Hot and Cold Grapefruit

1 large grapefruit (ruby red or yellow)
3 tbs sugar
2 tbs kirsch (cherry liqueur)
1 egg yolk
$^1/_2$ tsp vanilla extract
2 egg whites
salt
1 tbs candied fruit
1 tbs icing sugar
vanilla ice cream to serve

Halve the grapefruit and carefully separate the segments, preferably using a grapefruit knife. Lay the segments in a dish and mix with 2 tablespoons of sugar and some of the kirsch. Leave to stand in the fridge for 1 hour.

Take the empty shells of the grapefruit and clean them well, removing any remaining fibres. Fill them with ice, and chill in the deep freezer.

Whisk the egg yolk, the rest of the sugar and the vanilla extract into a pale cream. In a separate bowl, beat the egg whites with a pinch of salt until they stand in stiff peaks. Carefully fold the egg yolk mixture, the egg whites and the candied fruit together.

Remove the grapefruit shells from the freezer and divide the fruit segments between them. Put the egg mixture in an icing tube and squeeze it over the grapefruit using a star-shaped nozzle. Bake the grapefruit for a couple of minutes in an oven heated to 240°C (475°F), so that the egg mixture sets and browns. Serve immediately with ice cream.

Thrilling Coconut and Mango Cream

25 g (1 oz) grated coconut
125 ml ($^1/_2$ cup) warm milk
2 tbs tinned coconut cream
2 tbs white rum
2 sheets white gelatine
$^1/_2$ lemon or lime
1 large egg
$1^1/_2$ tbs sugar
125 g ($^1/_2$ cup) whipped cream
1 small mango
100 ml (scant $^1/_2$ cup) passion fruit juice

Cover the grated coconut in the milk and leave for a few hours for the coconut to absorb some of the milk. Combine the coconut cream and rum. Soak the gelatine in cold water for 5 minutes.

Meanwhile peel the zest of the lemon or lime, using a zester, and chop the ribbons into small pieces. Beat the egg, sugar and lemon or lime zest into a thick cream. Stir in the swollen coconut and the rum mixture.

Place the gelatine in a saucepan while it is still wet and dissolve in a little water over a low heat. Fold the gelatine into the cream. Leave the mixture to stand in the fridge until it is semi-set, then fold in the whipped cream. Leave the mixture to cool and set completely in the fridge for a further 3 hours. Peel the mango, cut into slices and steam in the passion fruit juice for a few minutes. Allow to cool and serve the fruit with the coconut cream on a plate.

Mint and Melon Wonder

30 g (1 oz) mint leaves
1–2 tbs honey
pinch of cardamom powder
3 sheets of white gelatine
$^1/_3$ honeydew melon
2 tbs lemon juice

For the wine sauce:
1 egg
2 tbs sugar
125 ml ($^1/_2$ cup) white wine

Put a few mint leaves aside and use the rest to brew tea in a teapot using 250 ml (2 cups) boiling water. Leave the leaves to brew for 10 minutes, and then pass the tea through a fine sieve. Add the honey and cardamom powder. Soften the gelatine in cold water for about 5 minutes, drain it well and dissolve it in the hot tea. Using a melon baller, carve balls out of the honeydew. Keep back six balls and put the rest into the tea along with some lemon juice and the rest of the mint leaves (leave a few leaves aside to garnish). Pour into two individual jelly (jello) moulds and leave to set in the fridge for 6 hours.

For the sauce, combine the egg, sugar and wine in a bain-marie and whisk into a thick foam. Turn out the jellies onto two large plates, pour some sauce over the jellies and garnish with mint leaves and melon balls.

Baked Banana Mélange

2 ripe bananas
2 tsp lemon juice
$^1/_2$ tbs butter
2 tbs orange juice
2 tsp dark rum (or more to taste)
2 tbs brown sugar
1 tsp cinnamon
4 tbs grated coconut

Peel the bananas and dribble lemon juice on them immediately to prevent them from going brown. Slice lengthways and lay in a greased baking tin.

Combine the orange juice, rum and sugar and pour over the bananas. Top with the cinnamon and coconut and bake in an oven pre-heated to 200°C (400°F) for 15 minutes. Serve while warm.

THE SPRING OF LOVE

There are more odd notions about drinking than there are about eating – for example, that by drinking something, the soul of the matter drunk is immediately absorbed. Nevertheless, alcohol and its intoxicating effect help to establish erotic contacts and intensify them.

APERITIFS

Adonis

Per glass:
30 ml (1 fluid oz) sherry
15 ml ($^1/_2$ fluid oz) vermouth rosso
15 ml ($^1/_2$ fluid oz) vermouth bianco
a couple of dashes of bitter orange

Mix all the ingredients thoroughly in a large glass over ice. Transfer the cocktail into pre-cooled cocktail glasses and serve.

South Sea Dream

Per glass:
50 ml ($1^2/_3$ fluid oz) coconut milk
2 tbs puréed fresh pineapple
20 ml ($^2/_3$ fluid oz) lime juice, freshly squeezed
10 ml ($^1/_3$ fluid oz) white rum
to garnish: $^1/_4$ slice pineapple, 1 mint leaf

Mix the ingredients with ice in a cocktail shaker and serve over crushed ice in a cocktail glass. Decorate with the pineapple slice and mint leaf.

Red Fire

Per glass:
20 ml (²/₃ fluid oz) orange liqueur
2 tbs lemon juice
4 very ripe puréed strawberries
champagne

Mix the ingredients well and add the champagne. Stir well and serve in a cocktail glass.

Raspberry Prosecco

Per glass:
2 tbs raspberries (puréed)
lemon balm leaves, finely chopped
Prosecco

Mix all the ingredients together and serve in a cocktail glass.

Angel's Delight

Per glass:
40 ml (1¹/₃ fluid oz) single cream
couple of dashes grenadine
20 ml (²/₃ fluid oz) triple sec
20 ml (²/₃ fluid oz) gin

Shake all the ingredients vigorously in a cocktail shaker with lots of ice, and pour into cocktail glasses.

Devil

Per glass:
20 ml (²/₃ fluid oz) dry vermouth
30 ml (1 fluid oz) port
dash of lemon juice
to garnish: lemon peel

Stir the ingredients well, over ice, and transfer to iced cocktail glasses. Decorate with lemon peel.

Knockout

Per glass:
20 ml ($^2/_3$ fluid oz) dry vermouth
20 ml ($^2/_3$ fluid oz) gin
couple of dashes of Pernod
dash of crème de menthe

Stir the ingredients well, and transfer to chilled martini glasses.

Leave it to Me

Per glass:
20 ml ($^2/_3$ fluid oz) dry vermouth
20 ml ($^2/_3$ fluid oz) gin
couple of dashes of lemon juice
couple of dashes of Maraschino
couple of dashes of apricot brandy

Shake in a cocktail shaker with ice and pour into a Martini glass.

Fallen Leaves

Per glass:
20 ml ($^2/_3$ fluid oz) vermouth rosso
10 ml ($^1/_3$ fluid oz) dry vermouth
20 ml ($^2/_3$ fluid oz) Calvados
dash of brandy
to garnish: lemon juice and peel

Stir the ingredients over a lot of ice and pour into a chilled cocktail glass. Sprinkle with lemon juice and add the peel.

Elderberries with Champagne

125 ml (^{1}/$_2$ cup) dry Riesling
100 ml (scant ^{1}/$_2$ cup) mineral water
100 ml (scant ^{1}/$_2$ cup) dry sparkling wine
juice of one lemon
1 clove
60 g (^{1}/$_2$ cup) elderberries with stems removed
250 ml (1 cup) champagne
to garnish:
raspberries, wild strawberries, 2 sprigs lemon balm

Mix the wine, mineral water, sparkling wine, lemon juice and clove together and boil. Allow the mixture to cool a little. Put the elderberries in a glass bottle and pour the warm liquid over them. Cover the bottle with a cloth and store in a cool place for one week. Strain the mixture through a fine sieve and freeze for 2–3 hours. While it is freezing, stir the mixture regularly, so that the ice crystals are not too big. Shortly before the sorbet completely sets, stir in 3–4 tablespoons of champagne and allow to freeze fully.

Fill a champagne bubble glass with scoops of sorbet and decorate with berries and lemon balm.

ALCOHOLIC DRINKS

Persian Love Potion

black tea
1 1/2 tbs sugar
plum slices
rum

Brew 500 ml (2 cups) black tea and leave to stand for 5 minutes. Mix in the sugar and leave to cool.

Place the plum slices in the tea glass, pour in a shot of rum and fill the glass with the cooled tea. Finally, add two ice cubes to each glass.

Spiced Coffee

3 tbs cocoa powder
2 tsp cinnamon
grated nutmeg
3 tbs honey
2 mugs hot coffee
40 ml (2/3 fluid oz) rum

Mix the cocoa, cinnamon, nutmeg and honey, adding one or two drops of water to help the ingredients mix. Stir into the coffee, and add rum to taste.

Celery Bowl

1 large stick celery
finely ground rock candy (to taste)
cognac (to taste)
2 bottles white wine

Clean the celery and cut into thin slices. Put in a glass bottle with the candy, and seal so that it is airtight. Leave to stand in a cool place. In the evening, pour in the cognac and leave to stand overnight. Before drinking, add the wine.

Ginger Beer

1 l (4 cups) beer
1 tbs ground ginger
$^1/_2$ tsp grated nutmeg
3 fresh eggs
honey

Mix the beer with the ginger and nutmeg in a saucepan and cook very slowly over a low heat. Meanwhile, beat the eggs, a little cold beer and some honey with a whisk until the mixture is foamy. Pour in the heated beer. Chill before serving, although this drink can also be enjoyed hot.

Banana Wine

3 kg (6 lb) over-ripe bananas, peeled
50 g (1 packet) fresh yeast
300 g (1¹/₂ cups) sugar

Purée the bananas. Finely grate the yeast and mix well with the sugar. Put everything in an earthenware pot and keep covered for three months. Filter the brew and serve chilled.

Spiced Wine

1 bottle burgundy wine
30 g (2 tbs) cinnamon
30 g (2 tbs) ground ginger
10 g (1 tbs) ground cloves
¹/₂ vanilla pod
400 g (2 cups) sugar

Put all the ingredients in a saucepan and warm slowly, making sure that the wine does not boil. Cover and leave to stand for 1 hour. Filter the wine through muslin before serving.

Ginseng Wine

500 ml (2 cups) rice wine
1 long ginseng root (fresh or dried)

Pour the rice wine over the ginseng root and leave to stand for a month. Drink one glass daily. Keep the ginseng in the wine until it is finished.

'Special' Tequila

handful of marijuana buds
1 piece fresh hemp root
1 chilli pepper
pinch of salt
1 bottle tequila

Add all the ingredients to the tequila and leave to stand for a week. Serve chilled, with freshly squeezed lemon juice. The solid ingredients should not be eaten.

Important note: In most countries possession of marijuana is illegal. It is the reader's responsibility to know the legal status of the possession of marijuana in the country they reside in. Neither the publisher nor the author condone illegal activities.

COCKTAILS

Bee's Kiss

Per glass:
20 ml (²/₃ fluid oz) cream
runny honey to taste
30 ml (1 fluid oz) white rum
10 ml (¹/₃ fluid oz) brown rum

Shake all the ingredients thoroughly in a cocktail shaker with ice and serve in a cocktail glass.

Between the Sheets

Per glass:
20 ml (²/₃ fluid oz) lemon juice
10 ml (¹/₃ fluid oz) triple sec
20 ml (²/₃ fluid oz) brandy
20 ml (²/₃ fluid oz) white rum

Put all the ingredients in a cocktail shaker with ice and shake thoroughly. Serve in a cocktail glass.

Green Leaves

Per glass:
mint leaves
20 ml (²/₃ fluid oz) crème de menthe
tonic water

Put the mint leaves in a large tumbler and pour the crème de menthe over them. Crush the leaves with a spoon, top with crushed ice, fill the glass with tonic water and stir.

Coconut Lips

Per glass:
60 ml (2 fluid oz) pineapple juice
40 ml (1¹/₃ fluid oz) single (light) cream
15 ml (¹/₂ fluid oz) coconut cream liqueur
10 ml (¹/₃ fluid oz) raspberry liqueur
to garnish: maraschino cherries, pineapple

Shake all the ingredients thoroughly in a cocktail shaker with lots of ice. Serve over crushed ice in a large tumbler. Decorate with cherries and pineapple.

Latin Lover

Per glass:
15 ml (¹/₂ fluid oz) lemon juice
20 ml (²/₃ fluid oz) Rose's lime cordial
50 ml (1¹/₃ fluid oz) pineapple juice
20 ml (²/₃ fluid oz) Cachaca
20 ml (²/₃ fluid oz) tequila
to garnish: pineapple

Mix all the ingredients with crushed ice and shake well in a cocktail shaker. Serve in a large tumbler with crushed ice. Garnish with pineapple.

Pick Me Up

Per glass:
10 ml (¹/₃ fluid oz) lemon juice
30 ml (1 fluid oz) brandy
dash of angostura bitters
dash of grenadine
few dashes of sugar syrup
champagne

Shake all the ingredients except the champagne thoroughly in a cocktail shaker with some ice. Pour into a champagne flute and top up with champagne.

Pina Colada

Per glass:
40 ml (1^1/$_3$ fluid oz) coconut milk
60 ml (2 fluid oz) pineapple juice
60 ml (2 fluid oz) white rum

U se an electric mixer to blend all the ingredients with some crushed ice and pour into a large tumbler.

TEA, COFFEE AND COCOA

Fresh, Enlivening Tea

500 g (1 cup) fresh tea (twigs and leaves) from Asia
2 l (8 cups) still mineral water, cold

Wash the tea, and add to the mineral water. Bring to the boil and cook on a rolling boil for 30 minutes. Fill a teapot with it. The tea leaves will make up to three brews. The tea should be drunk without sugar.

Chinese Ginger Tea

For two cups:
4–6 pieces ginger root
2 tsp sugar

Place the ginger in four cups of water and boil until half the liquid is left. Add sugar, and drink while it is hot.

Ginseng Tea

1 tbs ginseng root
1 tbs ginger root
1 tbs liquorice
1 date
honey or sugar

Bring all the ingredients except the honey or sugar to the boil and leave to stand. Strain the tea and sweeten with honey or sugar. Drink once daily for aphrodisiac effect.

Vietnamese Sweet Talking Tea

1 l (4 cups) still mineral water
2 sticks sugarcane
5 sticks liquorice
2 mint sprigs
1 tsp black tea

Bring the water to the boil. Chop the sugarcane and liquorice. Wash and dry the mint sprigs. Place all the ingredients in a teapot and pour in the boiling water. Leave to brew for 5 minutes.

Moroccan Peppermint Tea

$^1/_2$ sprig fresh mint
sugar or honey

Put the mint leaves in a glass (there should be plenty of leaves) and pour in boiling water. Sweeten according to taste.

Pineapple Tea

6 tsp black tea
1 fresh pineapple, cut into slices
juice of one lemon
750 ml (3 cups) still mineral water
candied ginger, finely chopped

Brew the tea for 5 minutes and leave to go cold. Cube four slices of pineapple and squeeze lemon juice onto them. Add the tea to the pineapple and chill. Before serving, add the mineral water and the ginger.

Iced Tea with Ginger

12 tsp black tea
1 l (4 cups) still mineral water
brown sugar
1 lemon, sliced
pickled ginger

Brew the tea for 5 minutes, using the mineral water. Fill tall glasses two-thirds full with ice cubes and pour the tea over them. Sweeten according to taste with brown sugar. Garnish the glasses with lemon slices and sliced ginger.

Cardamom Coffee

1 heaped tsp ground filter coffee
1 heaped tsp cardamom seeds
honey or sugar
milk

Mix the coffee and the cardamom seeds and brew in boiling water. Sweeten according to taste and add milk.

Mexican Cocoa

1 l (4 cups) milk
2 vanilla pods
4 tbs cocoa
2 tbs honey
4 tbs sugar
chilli powder
salt

Slowly heat the milk on a low heat with the vanilla pods. After 10 minutes, remove the vanilla, slit the pods open and scrape out the core. Mix the seeds with the cocoa and 250 millilitres (1 cup) water and pour into the hot milk. Add the honey and sugar, along with a pinch of chilli powder and salt. Take the pan from the stove and whisk the cocoa until it is foamy.

Anti-stress Cocoa

5 heaped tsp cocoa
1–2 tsp cinnamon
2 pinches cardamom powder
1 pinch clove powder
$^1/_2$ vanilla bean pod
1 pinch chilli (according to taste)
4–6 tsp honey

Bring all the ingredients to the boil in 500 millilitres (2 cups) water and boil for 5 minutes.

MISCELLANEOUS DRINKS

Guarana Drink

guarana seeds
1 l (4 cups) boiling water

Crush a handful of guarana seeds in a pestle and mortar and add to the water. After 5–10 minutes, strain the seeds out and drink. The seeds can be used up to four times to make tea.

Honey Water

1 sprig rosemary
1 sprig sage
1 sprig rue
watercress
250 g (¹/₂ cup) fresh honey

Place the herbs in a glass filled with honey and leave for three months, taking care to seal the glass. To prepare the drink, brew 1 teaspoon of the honey in boiling water. Drink regularly.

Celery Water

1 tsp celery seeds

Leave the celery seeds to stand in two glasses of water for 8 hours. Strain the seeds out and drink daily.

Krishna's Drink

2 cups almonds
2 cups blueberries
2–4 tbs maple syrup (according to taste)
4 cups still mineral water

Soak the almonds overnight. The next day, put them in boiling water for 90 seconds. Remove the brown skin and chop the nuts. Slowly add the mineral water. Purée the blueberries through a sieve and into the almonds. Sweeten with maple syrup.

OBJECTS OF DESIRE – MENUS FOR LOVERS

SPRING FEVER MENU

Asparagus Salad

Tempestuous Turbot in Riesling Cream Sauce

Rhubarb and Strawberry Fool

Asparagus Salad

150 g (5 oz) green beans (string beans)
50 g (2 oz) fresh button mushrooms
salt and pepper
1 tbs lemon juice
1 carrot
200 g (8 oz) freshly cooked asparagus
2 tbs cold pressed virgin olive oil

Cook the beans in salted water for 5–7 minutes, drain and rinse in cold water so that the beans keep their colour. Clean the mushrooms, cut into thin slices and season with salt, pepper and lemon juice. Peel the carrot and cut into long fine straws. Cut the asparagus into pieces approximately 4 centimetres (1½ inches) long. Trim the tops and bottoms of the beans and slice in half. Combine the beans, mushrooms and carrot, place the mixture next to the asparagus on the plate and drizzle with olive oil.

Tempestuous Turbot in Riesling Cream Sauce

2 fillets turbot
lemon juice
2 shallots
$^1/_2$ bunch chervil
100 g (1 oz or 1 stick) cold butter
100 ml (scant $^1/_2$ cup) dry white wine (preferably Riesling)
1 large beef tomato
80 g (3 oz) button mushrooms
100 ml (scant $^1/_2$ cup) single (light) cream
salt and freshly ground black pepper
3 tbs crème fraîche

Wash the fish in cold water, dab dry and season with lemon juice. Finely chop the shallots and chervil. Take 30 grams (1 ounce) of the butter, melt it in a pan, fry the shallots until they are translucent and then add the fish fillets. Add the chervil, wine and 3 tablespoons of water and steam with the lid on the pan for 12–15 minutes.

Meanwhile, remove the skin and seeds from the tomato and cut the flesh into slices. Clean the mushrooms and slice them. Remove the fish from the pan and keep warm. Pour the cream into the cooking juices and bring to the boil. Add the tomato and mushrooms and cook over a low heat. Dice the cold butter and whisk it in a little at a time until the sauce is thick and creamy. Season with salt and pepper, add the crème fraîche and cook for a couple more minutes. Pour the sauce over the fish and garnish with a few chervil leaves. Serve with tagliatelle.

Rhubarb and Strawberry Fool

450 g (1 lb) rhubarb
100 g (3¹/₂ oz) sugar
2 sheets white gelatine
100 g (3¹/₂ oz) strawberries
a little icing sugar
1 egg white
125 ml (¹/₂ cup) whipping cream
2 sprigs mint

Peel the rhubarb and cut the stalks into small pieces. Place them in a saucepan and sprinkle three-quarters of the sugar over them. Leave to stand for 2 hours and then cook until it is so soft that it has turned to a mush.

Soak the gelatine in cold water for 5 minutes, drain well and dissolve the sheet in the rhubarb. Leave to cool, until the mixture has set. Meanwhile clean and halve the strawberries, keeping back two attractive strawberries that still have their stems for the garnish. Sweeten the rest of the strawberries with a little icing sugar.

Beat the egg white until it stands in stiff peaks and fold in the rest of the sugar. Next, fold into the cooled rhubarb mixture. Beat the cream until it is stiff and fold carefully into the rhubarb mousse. Mix in the strawberry halves. Pour the mixture into two tall glasses and garnish with the whole strawberries and the mint leaves.

SUMMER LOVIN' MENU

Gazpacho

Pampered Pigeon and Peas

Vanilla Ice Cream with Flambéed Raspberry Sauce

Gazpacho

1 large fresh gherkin
1 very ripe tomato
1 red pepper
1 egg yolk
2 tbs olive oil
1 tbs sunflower oil
1 tsp red wine vinegar
salt and freshly ground black pepper
1 small slice white bread
1 clove garlic

Peel, halve and de-seed the gherkin. Boil the tomato briefly, remove its skin, halve it and remove the seeds. Remove the core and seeds from the red pepper and slice the flesh in half. Finely dice a quarter of the vegetables and purée the rest of them in a blender. Beat the egg yolk, half the olive oil, the sunflower oil and vinegar until it forms a thick cream. Add the vegetable purée, season with salt and pepper and leave to chill in the fridge for 1–2 hours.

Finely dice the white bread. Heat the rest of the olive oil in a pan and fry the garlic until it is golden brown. Remove the garlic and then fry the bread to make garlic croutons.

Serve the soup in two bowls and garnish with the diced vegetables and croutons.

Pampered Pigeon and Peas

2 young pigeons
salt and freshly ground black pepper
2 slices streaky bacon
1 tbs melted butter

For the stuffing:
¹/₂ bread roll
2 tbs poultry stock
100 g (4 oz) chicken liver
2 rashers lean bacon
1 large shallot
1 tbs butter
1 tsp chopped parsley
1 tbs chopped herbs (basil, thyme, marjoram)
1 egg
1 tsp chopped pistachios

For the sauce:
1 shallot
1 tsp butter
100 ml (scant ¹/₂ cup) Madeira
200 ml (generous ³/₄ cup) poultry juices

Prepare the pigeons for cooking – remove the neck and wings and loosen the skin from the neck and over the breast. Wash the birds and dry well.

For the stuffing, finely chop the bread roll, pour the stock over the bread and leave for a few minutes to soak. Squeeze any excess stock from the bread. Remove the livers and hearts from the pigeons. Halve the hearts and finely chop the chicken liver. Finely dice the bacon and the shallot. Fry the liver, hearts, bacon and shallot in the butter. Add the parsley and some of the herbs and fry for a little longer. Take half of the mixture and mix with the bread roll and purée. Mix the egg, pistachios and the rest of the herbs with the remaining giblet mixture.

Season the insides of the pigeons with salt and pepper. Fill the abdominal cavities with one stuffing, and place the other under the loosened skin over the breasts. Place a slice of bacon over each bird and, using kitchen string, sew the birds up so that the stuffing is secured and the bacon is fixed to the pigeon breast. Fry the birds in hot butter until they are golden brown, turning them frequently. Remove and keep warm. Pour any excess fat from the pan, and add 4 tablespoons of water to the remaining cooking juices to make the sauce.

For the sauce, chop up the pigeon wings and the shallot and fry them in butter. Douse frequently with the Madeira, so that a *jus* is created. Strain the *jus* through a sieve, season with salt and pepper and add the rest of the herbs.

Remove and discard the bacon from the pigeons, and place the birds on two plates. Pour the sauce over them and serve with side dishes of peas and duchesse potatoes.

Duchesse Potatoes

225 g (8 oz) well-boiled potatoes
1 egg
grated nutmeg
salt
2 tsp butter
1 egg yolk
1 tbs cream

Place the potatoes in a baking tin and allow them to dry out in a hot oven for a few minutes – all the moisture from boiling must be evaporated. Mash the dry potatoes and work in the egg, nutmeg and salt. Stir in 1 tablespoon of butter.

Smear a baking tray with butter. Spoon the potato into an icing tube with a large star-shaped nozzle and squeeze potato rosettes onto the tray. Mix the egg yolk and the cream and brush onto the tops of the rosettes. Bake the potatoes in an oven pre-heated to 180°C (350°F) until the tops are golden.

Vanilla Ice Cream with Flambéed Raspberry Sauce

200 g (8 oz) raspberries
1 tbs lemon juice
2 tbs sugar
1 tbs raspberry conserve
2 tbs raspberry liqueur
2 portions vanilla ice cream

Mix the raspberries with the lemon juice, sugar and conserve. Warm the mixture over a low heat and add the liqueur. Once the sauce is warm enough, flambé until the alcohol has burnt off, and then serve over the ice cream.

AUTUMNAL LONGING MENU

Snails in Herb Sauce

Wild Mushroom Consommé

Make-me-swoon Venison Medallions with Mashed Celery

Cheese Plate

Snails in Herb Sauce

3 tbs butter
1 tbs double (heavy) cream
1 tbs white wine
1 clove garlic, crushed
1 tsp cloves, finely chopped
1 tbs mixed herbs (chervil, tarragon, thyme, rosemary)
pepper
1 piece toast
1 tomato
12 tinned snails, their shells removed

Melt 1 tablespoon of butter with the cream, wine, garlic and herbs, warm and set aside.

Very finely dice the slice of toast and fry in 1 tablespoon of butter to make croutons. Blanch the tomato in boiling water for a few minutes and peel the skin. Then halve it, remove the seeds and finely dice the flesh. Salt it and fry lightly in some butter. Heat the snails in the juice from the tin and when warmed, drain them well.

Fill two ramekins with the snails and sauce and garnish with the diced tomato and croutons. Serve hot with a baguette.

Wild Mushroom Consommé

25 g (¹/₂ cup) dried wild mushrooms
500 ml (2 cups) veal stock
1 egg white
75 g (1 cup) fresh wild mushrooms
1 tbs oil
salt and black pepper
2 tbs chopped chives

Soak the dried mushrooms in lukewarm stock for 15 minutes. Lightly beat the egg white and stir into the stock. Bring to the boil then simmer, covered, for 15 minutes.

Line a sieve with muslin and sieve the stock, without stirring or pressing it through; the stock should be crystal clear. Clean the fresh mushrooms and slice them. Fry them briefly in hot oil and season with salt and pepper.

Place the mushroom slices in pre-warmed bowls. Season the consommé, reheat it without allowing it to boil, pour into the bowls and garnish with chives. Serve with fresh crusty bread.

Make-me-swoon Venison Medallions

4 venison medallions (about 2–3cm /1 in thick)
1 tsp grated ginger
salt and freshly ground black pepper
1 small onion
1 small carrot
1 tbs oil
25 g (1 oz or ¼ stick) butter
250 ml (1 cup) game stock
2 tbs double (heavy) cream

Rub the meat with the ginger, salt and pepper. Peel the onion and carrot and finely dice them. Heat the oil and butter in a pan, and fry the medallions over a medium heat for 2–3 minutes on each side (the meat should still be juicy and pink on the inside). Remove the meat from the pan, wrap it in aluminium foil and keep warm.

Sweat the onion and carrot in the meat fat, add the stock and reduce the mixture to half its original volume. Purée the sauce, strain it through a sieve back into the pan and stir in the cream. Cook the sauce briefly and season with a pinch of sugar, salt and pepper. Arrange the meat on the plates and pour any juices from the meat back into the sauce. Serve the sauce separately, along with a side dish of mashed celery.

Mashed Celery

250 g (10 oz) celery
2 tbs double (heavy) cream
1 tbs burnt butter
salt
1 tbs whipped cream

Peel the celery and cut into small pieces. Cook it in salted water until it is soft. Pour off the water, add the cream and then purée with a potato masher. Mix in the butter and season with salt. Before serving, fold in the whipped cream.

WINTER STORMS

Marinated King Prawns

Beef Fillet Fanfare

Apple and Potato Gratin

Baked Apples with Custard

Marinated King Prawns

2 limes
2 oranges
salt
1 tsp sugar
1 small red onion
1 red chilli
1 small beef tomato
8 green king prawns
1 bunch flat parsley, chopped
fresh coriander, chopped

Grate the orange and lime rinds. Juice all four fruit into a large bowl and add the rind. Season with some salt and the sugar and mix well.

Peel the onion, cut into wafer-thin rings and add them to the juice. Remove the chilli seeds and discard. Chop the rest of the chilli very finely and add to the bowl.

Boil the tomato for a few minutes and remove its skin. Halve it and discard the seeds. Finely dice the flesh and add to the marinade, along with the parsley and coriander.

Bring some salted water to the boil, add the prawns and cook in a covered pan on a low heat for around 4 minutes. Remove the prawns and rinse them in cold water to prevent them cooking further. Leaving the tails on, remove the shells and carefully remove the vein with a toothpick. If desired, the prawns can be cut lengthways in half before swirling them through the marinade.

Serve on a bed of salad, with a little marinade poured over the prawns. Garnish with rest of parsley and coriander.

Beef Fillet Fanfare

2 fillets of beef (each weighing 100 g (3½ oz))
salt and freshly ground black pepper
200 g (7 oz) chicken liver
1 tbs raisins
2 tbs cognac
2 tbs shallots, finely chopped
4 tbs butter
100 ml (½ cup) stock
2 tbs Madeira
1 bay leaf
thyme
1 tsp tomato purée
½ tsp meat stock cube
cayenne pepper

Season the meat with the pepper. Cut the chicken liver into thin slices. Wash the raisins and leave them to soak in the cognac. Sweat the shallots for 2–3 minutes in ½ a tablespoon of butter. Add the stock and cook over a high heat. Stir in the Madeira, add the bay leaf and slowly reduce the liquid to half its volume over a low heat. Flash fry the fillets in 1 tablespoon of foaming butter to seal them, season with salt and set aside on a warmed plate. Heat ½ a tablespoon of butter in the same pan and fry the liver for a minute or two. Remove the pan from the stove and season with salt, pepper and thyme.

Add the raisins and cognac to the cooking juices and stir in the tomato purée, crumbled stock cube and the cooking juices from the steaks. Bring to the boil for a moment, and then remove from the heat and whisk 2 tablespoons of butter into the sauce until it melts. Season the sauce with salt, a pinch of cayenne pepper and thyme. Mix the liver into the sauce and pour over the two steaks on the serving plates.

Serve with Apple and Potato Gratin (see page 206).

Apple and Potato Gratin

225 g (8 oz) boiled potatoes
2 small cooking apples
1 tsp butter
salt and freshly ground black pepper
10 sage leaves, coarsely chopped
100 ml (scant ¹/₂ cup) whipped cream
2 tbs olive oil

Peel the potatoes and apples and remove the apple cores. Slice the potatoes and apples very thinly and place them in layers in a greased Pyrex dish. Season with salt and pepper and sprinkle the sage leaves on top. Mix the cream and oil together and spread over the top. Bake in an oven pre-heated to 225°C (430°F) for 20 minutes.

Baked Apples with Custard

2 medium–sized apples
1 tbs marzipan
1 tbs rum
1 tsp chopped almonds
1 tbs chopped pistachios
1 tsp butter
125 ml ($^1/_2$ cup) medium white wine

For the sauce:
5 tbs milk
5 tbs single (light) cream
3 tbs sugar
$^1/_2$ vanilla bean pod
1 egg yolk
1 egg

Warm the milk, cream, half the sugar and the seeds from the vanilla pod. Bring the mixture slowly to the boil, stirring often. Whisk the egg yolk, egg and the rest of the sugar until foamy. Place the hot milk mixture in a bain-marie, and then gradually combine the milk and the egg mixture until the sauce thickens. Take care that the water bath does not become too hot, or the sauce will curdle. Once the sauces have combined and slightly thickened, remove from the heat to cool.

Remove the apple cores using a corer, so that the apples still look neat. Combine the marzipan, rum, almonds and half the pistachios. Lay the apples in an oven-proof dish and fill the holes where the core was with the mixture. Lay small flecks of butter on top of the apples so that they do not dry out during baking.

Bake in an oven pre-heated to 180°C (350°F), occasionally basting the apples with the wine.

Arrange the two apples on plates, pour over the vanilla sauce and garnish with the remaining pistachios.

EXOTIC LOVE MENU

Happy Rolls

Avocado Soup

Vietnamese Coconut Rice

Burmese Chicken Curry

Tropical Fruit Salad

Happy Rolls

1 egg
100 g ($^1/_4$ lb) very lean pork neck fillet
1 tbs butter
4 sheets rice paper
2 scampi
50 g (1 cup) fresh soya beansprouts
$^1/_4$ fresh salad gherkin
head of lettuce
$^1/_2$ bunch chives
$^1/_2$ bunch mint
$^1/_2$ bunch coriander
1 tbs chopped peanuts
125 ml ($^1/_2$ cup) hoi–sin sauce

Beat the egg, cook as an omelette and leave to go cold. Fry the pork fillet for 15 minutes and slice into wafer-thin pieces. Meanwhile, moisten the rice paper with a spritzer and lay on a damp cloth. Cook the scampi in their shells, remove the shells and halve them lengthways. Wash the beansprouts. Cut the gherkin into thin slices and separate the lettuce leaves. Cut the omelette into strips.

Put four lettuce leaves on the serving plates and fill with the following ingredients: pork, beansprouts, scampi, gherkin slices, omelette strips, chives, mint, coriander and peanuts. Season with a pinch of salt.

Serve with the hoi-sin sauce for dipping.

Avocado Soup

1 ripe avocado
1 cup crème fraîche
1 small onion, finely chopped
2 cloves garlic, crushed
salt and pepper
1 tsp Tabasco sauce
500 ml (2 cups) hot chicken stock
1 tbs fresh dill (or other fresh herbs)

Open the avocado, remove the meat and mash it finely with a fork. Add the crème fraîche and mix it in well. Mix the onion and garlic thoroughly into the purée. Season with salt, pepper and Tabasco. Pour in the chicken stock and simmer over a low heat for 15 minutes. Before serving, garnish with dill.

Vietnamese Coconut Rice

200 g (7 oz) long grain rice
1 tin coconut milk
salt
5 cloves
$^1/_2$ stick cinnamon

Wash the rice in cold water and drain dry. Cover with 250 millilitres (1 cup) water and bring to the boil. Stir in the coconut milk and a large pinch of salt. Simmer, covered, for another 3 minutes. Then cook over a high heat for 2 minutes so that a lot of excess moisture evaporates. Making sure that the spices are distributed evenly throughout the rice, add the cloves and cinnamon and cook on a low heat for a further 20 minutes. Take the saucepan off the heat, carefully stir the rice and keep covered for 15 minutes. Before serving, remove the cinnamon and cloves.

Burmese Chicken Curry

1 small chicken or chicken pieces
$^1/_4$ tsp saffron
1 tbs soy sauce
2 tbs curry powder
$^1/_2$ tsp chilli powder
2 onions
3 cloves garlic
oil
3 bay leaves
1 tsp ground cinnamon
salt

Divide the chicken into portions. Season with the saffron, soy sauce and curry powder. Mix the chilli, onion and garlic. In a saucepan heat the oil and fry the onion mixture. Add the chicken and fry until golden brown. Add the bay leaves, cinnamon, salt and 625 millilitres ($2^1/_2$ cups) water. Simmer on a low heat for approximately one hour.

Tropical Fruit Salad

A mixture of your favourite tropical fruits, which may include: lychees; fresh pineapple; banana; papaya; mangoes; star fruit
1 tbs runny honey
2 tbs grated coconut

Prepare the fruit. Mix in the honey and garnish with the coconut.

INDEX

Index

Index